the WarriHER's Pl▶ybook

on Well-Being and Self-Advocacy

Also by Author

O-Syndrome: When Work is 24/7 and You're Not (2017)

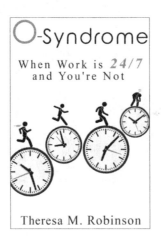

Overcoming Gender Inequity: Real, Raw, Unapologetic Stories, Tips & Strategies (2019)

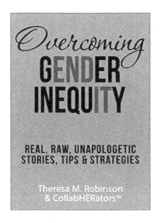

the WarriHER's Playbook

on Well-Being and Self-Advocacy

Theresa M. Robinson

with

Baylie Robinson

Carrie Sechel

ChrisTiana ObeySumner

Harriet K. Harty

Jemia Young

Laura McGuire

Mayerland Harris

Nani Shin

Rhoda Harriet Khataba

Sara Sanders Gardner

Published by:

Master Trainer TMR

Master Trainer TMR & Associates, LLC

The WarriHER's Playbook on Well-Being and Self-Advocacy
Copyright © 2019
Master Trainer TMR & Associates, LLC

All rights reserved. No part of this book may be reproduced by any
mechanical, photographic, or electronic process, or in the form of
phonographic recording; nor may it be stored in a retrieval system,
transmitted, or otherwise copied for public or private use
without the prior written permission of the publisher.

Master Trainer TMR & Associates, LLC
Houston, TX
info@MasterTrainerTMR.com

Theresa M. Robinson, primary author

ISBN 978-0-9988420-6-6 Paperback

First Edition

This is a work of nonfiction. Some names and
identifying details have been changed.

Dedication

To Eloise Barber and Thelma Robinson,
whose badass-ery continues to inspire generations.

To all warriHERs on the front line,
I see you. I hear you.

Table of Contents

Part II: Self-Advocacy

"Caring for myself is not self-indulgence;
it is self-preservation, and that
is an act of political warfare."

Audre Lorde
1934 - 1992

Preface

When I facilitate workshops on my first two books—*O-Syndrome: When Work is 24/7 and You're Not* and *Overcoming Gender Inequity: Real, Raw, Unapologetic Stories, Tips & Strategies*—I consistently hear from women saying they want more. They need more. Women are not only clamoring to tell their stories; they are eager for practical solutions that take into account the intersection of women's multiple identities. Many workshops end with post-session conversations, coaching, and new friendships.

As a result, I realized that I wanted to support women even further by developing a new resource to continue their journey in practical ways—long after the workshops have ended. So, in the early months of 2019, with the concept born, I began work on a project to supplement my first two books. It would be a workbook—filled with introspective exercises, activities, and numerous additional insights. I dubbed it *The WarriHER's Playbook*, for short.

The new Playbook would have a dual focus: first, women making self-care a priority, and second, women speaking up and speaking out for themselves in the face of gender bias and inequity. But as I started to wrap up the project, I realized that it was still missing something. That's when it hit me! What kind of WarriHER Playbook would it be without the combined wisdom and experience of a diverse tribe of warriHERs? From that point on, the project was infused with new life, organically growing out of the collabHERator experiences I had enjoyed while writing my second book.

I remain convinced that when women unite and support one another, we grow stronger individually and are collectively fortified to advance the work. I'm both thrilled and proud to share this latest collaboration with you and with the following ten amazing warriHER co-authors. They, like I, have heeded the call to support women in becoming better and stronger versions of ourselves.

10 WarriHER Co-Authors

Baylie Robinson
Senior Account Executive, Blogger
Author of *Life Lessons College Failed to Teach You*

Carrie Sechel
Owner, Consultant, Speaker
Carrie Sechel, LLC
Author of best seller *BASE Jump*

ChrisTiana ObeySumner, MNPL
CEO, Epiphanies of Equity: Education and Consulting
Founding E.D., Eleanor Elizabeth Institute for Black Empowerment

Harriet K. Harty
Chief Human Resources Officer

Jemia Young, MBA
Certified Diversity & Inclusion Practitioner, Creative, Blogger

Laura McGuire, Ed. D.
Sexologist, Consultant
The National Center for Equity and Agency
Author of *The Sexual Misconduct Handbook: Consent and Conduct on Higher Education Campuses* and *Creating Cultures of Consent: A Guide for Parents and Educators*

Mayerland Harris, MBA, SPHR
Group Vice President of Human Resources

Nani Shin
President, Harmony Partners Consulting
Founder, W.E. Tribe

Rhoda Harriet Khataba
Founder & Executive Director, Her Story Matters

Sara Sanders Gardner
Director, Neurodiversity Navigators Program, Bellevue College, WA
Trainer, Consultant, Autistic at Work

Introduction

warriHER

/wôr' ē hər/

an inspiringly brave, fiercely resilient, stereotype-busting, tenaciously courageous, relentlessly determined woman who, while prioritizing her well-being, actively engages in both solo-combat and group-combat to champion gender equity by strategically employing weapons in her arsenal, such as voice, platform, mentorship, education, advocacy, activism

In this fast-paced 24/7 digital world of ours, with all of its pressures and demands, do you sometimes feel as though you're losing yourself? Do you feel like you're losing what anchors you to what's real and true or question if you can even recognize what's real and true about your life? Do you ask yourself what matters most to you? Do you harbor concerns about your well-being or question if it can co-exist with high performance? Are you struggling to contain your rage over the daily assault of micro-aggressions? Do you struggle with how to speak up and speak out for yourself when the gender equity deck is statistically stacked against you?

Has your best (or only) solution been to do what women have been taught to do for ages, namely, suck it up, smile, and then complain to anybody who'll listen?

If so, how's that working for you?

This is not the day to suck it up and smile.

And this is not that kind of playbook.

There's no denying that external factors pose great challenges. Sometimes, however, our greatest moments come when we tackle not what's outside but what's inside. While we continue to do the collective work of supporting and advancing gender equity, we must first commit to doing the foundational self-work. Ours is not a world that relishes the value of deep introspection and inner conviction. Performance and profit are often elevated above values and character. Many have traded the power of stillness for the lure of busy-ness.

Consider the context of the modern world. Technology has given each of us the "opportunity" to work 24 hours a day, 7 days a week, 365 days a year. The only exception is leap year; then it's 366 days a year. This is in stark contrast to the misguided belief and prediction that technology would make our lives easier. In many ways, it has. But without boundaries and hard stops, work is a continuous and endless cycle that, if we allow it to, can consume us.

Is it any surprise that those between the ages of 30 and 45 are reportedly the most overworked and exhausted demographic? These are the years that careers are in their prime, characterized by promotions and increased responsibilities. The responsibilities of raising children dovetail with mounting concerns for aging or ailing parents. This sandwich generation—caught between their children and their parents—often achieve success at great cost.

For many, achieving great career success often goes hand-in-hand with declining health, strained relationships, or unhappiness. I've met with women in corporate and listened to their laments all too often. I've said this before—and it continues to be validated across a variety of industries: the way women characterize "the work of work" is different than the way men characterize it. The way women characterize their well-being differs from the way men characterize their well-being. The way women characterize their role as working parents differs from the way men characterize their role as working parents.

And finally, the term "working mother" is more common and more readily referenced than is the term "working father." Serious question: Has a magazine called *Working Father* ever even existed? Has even the idea for this kind of magazine ever existed?

The way women experience the consequences of busy-ness is informed by our identities—as women, as mothers, as daughters, as sisters. Consider this. Do you bear the primary responsibility for child-rearing, household chores, and dinner preparation though you're in a dual-career relationship? Have you ever been the recipient of "mommy-shaming" or felt the weight of "mommy-guilt"? Are you expected to be the nurturer of members of your extended family? Do you feel conflicted or confused by simultaneously feeling pride and shame over being perceived as a "superwoman"? Have you ever felt compelled to weigh the impact of starting a family on your career? Do you sometimes find yourself so busy that you neglect your need for sleep and rest, yet you somehow manage to take care of everyone else?

This persistent state is coupled with what I call *O-Syndrome*—being overworked, overstressed, overburdened, overloaded, overcommitted, over-obligated, overtired, overwhelmed, overextended, and overscheduled. The combination threatens the very fiber of our values and belief systems and propels us toward a crisis of well-being.

Because O-Syndrome for women is exacerbated by patriarchal "norms" and systems of oppression, gender-bias, and discrimination, it can cause tremendous internal pressure and stress. Dr. Valerie Rein, a psychologist and mental health expert, refers to it as PSD, Patriarchy Stress Disorder™. She posits that "women in a patriarchal society, experience 'power outages' caused by micro-triggers that make it feel unsafe for us to be fully present in our full authentic expression." Dr. Valerie goes on to say that "these power outages lead to us working much harder than we need to, running on a significantly lower power supply than we otherwise would have." Her work underscores why it's critical for us as women to both take care of ourselves and arm ourselves to take on the larger systemic issues that impact us.

This playbook is designed just for you, no matter your career stage, no matter your industry, no matter your family status. Because you are in combat to win your life back, the exercises and activities provided are called *Battle Plans*. And woven throughout the book are the voices of ten warriHERs who share their personal wisdom and experience with you. Their words are here to help you to stay grounded as you activate your fighting spirit in a battle for your well-being.

Ready to get armored up? Let's do this!

Part I: Well-Being

well-being

/wel ˈbē iŋ/

a state of thriving in health and happiness such that one has the best experience of life both at home and at work

Battleground

8 September 2008.

Contrary to what is my habit, I answered a call on my cellphone from an unrecognizable number. The voice on the other end of the line would utter words that would forever alter several lives.

"Mrs. Robinson. This is Dr. Saboda calling from Washington Hospital Center in Washington, D.C. Your mother has suffered a massive stroke…"

His voice kept going as I lapsed into shock.

What is he talking about? How did he get my number? My mother and I don't know a Saboda. I think he has the wrong number. Did he just say that my mother surfed a missing coat? What?!

My memory of that day remains shrouded in a part of my consciousness that I still can't fully access.

After the 48 hours it took to "fully" process the news that my mother would either not survive or survive as a non-verbal person living with full-body paralysis, my reaction was to totally give up eating beef. I know. Strange and puzzling. Maybe not so strange when one considers that my usual control issues skyrocketed to a whole new level. My decision to give up beef was my way of mediating my emotions and handling my mother's stroke, all while attempting to exert control and order over my own life and my health in a way in which my mother had failed to do with hers.

You see, she had known prior to September 8 that she was at risk based on her lifestyle choices and history of blood clots. Yet she remained stubborn and steadfast in her decision to ignore her doctor's advice and the pleas of my two sisters and me to take better care of herself. A generous soul her entire life, my mother was the ultimate giver to everyone except to herself.

My mother survived her stroke and now requires maximum assistance with activities of daily living (ADL). What she had failed to do for herself, she is now "forced" to have others do for her. Paralyzed from the waist down and mobile by virtue of a wheelchair, she is living out the harshest of lessons.

Her experience and her lesson also continue to be mine.

Living in a state of well-being is available to each of us, whether we're introverted, extroverted, or ambiverted. Whether we're a C-suite executive, an entrepreneur, or an individual contributor. Whether we're Gen Z, Gen Y, Gen X, or Baby Boomer.

Well-being is a skill that can be learned, practiced, and mastered if it is prioritized. Any serious pursuit of well-being requires intention, especially because of life's constant demands. The pay-off is the opportunity to experience the best of life. Not merely surviving. Thriving. True well-being gives us fulfillment at home and at work; we don't have to feel as though we're forced to choose between one or the other.

Without well-being, we slip into O-Syndrome as our normative state. O-Syndrome, which I introduced in my first book, *O-Syndrome: When Work is 24/7 and You're Not*, is characterized by heightened busy-ness and exhaustion. It refers to being over-worked, overstressed, overburdened, overloaded, over-committed, over-obligated, overtired, overwhelmed, over-extended, over-scheduled, and just plain over it! Sound familiar? If you rack up enough "overs," you enter burnout territory—a pervasive sense of hopelessness about your situation, an inability to feel rested no matter the amount of sleep you get, and an overriding cynicism about everything.

So, test yourself. Place a check (√) beside each aspect of O-Syndrome that resonates with what your experience has been in the last six months to a year.

_____   Overworked—Juggling multiple balls in the air for ten hours a day or more.

_____   Overstressed—Feeling that one or more balls are in danger of falling, doing everything possible to prevent it, all while still maintaining all other balls in the air.

_____   Overburdened—Still keeping multiple balls in the air even though they have increased in size and weight.

_____   Overloaded—Taking on one or more additional balls while still keeping all balls in the air.

_____   Overcommitted—Helping others keep *their* multiple balls in the air while you maintain your own multiple balls in the air.

_____   Over-obligated—Being available, regardless of the day or time, to help others keep their multiple balls in the air while you still keep your own multiple balls in the air.

_____   Overtired—Attending to your multiple balls leaves you with little to no time to care for yourself and little leftover energy to engage with loved ones and friends.

_____   Overwhelmed—Thinking constantly about your present and future balls, the weight of your multiple balls, and the strength and skill required to maintain your multiple balls in the air.

_____   Overextended—Having only two hands to keep your multiple balls in the air when more hands and longer arms are clearly required.

_____   Overscheduled—Blocking off meeting and teleconference times on your calendar, even across multiple time zones, in order to strategize about collective balls, troubleshoot collective balls, plan for bigger balls, etc.

_____   Over it!—With fatalistic resignation, you go through the motions of keeping your multiple balls in the air.

Battle Plan #1 Confronting FOBO (Fear of Burn Out)

Now that you've walked through the defining characteristics of O-Syndrome, in your own words, how would you characterize burnout? Record your thoughts:

_____

_____

_____

_____

_____

_____

Using your own characterization of burnout, indicate with an (x) where you are currently on this continuum:

Burnout   O-Syndrome   Well-Being

-------------------*

What is your reaction to your current state?

_____

_____

_____

_____

What, if anything, concerns you about your current state?

_____

_____

_____

_____

_____

What would be—or what is—the impact of burnout on your life professionally and personally?

_____

_____

_____

_____

_____

_____

Battle Plan #2 Prioritizing the "Me" in Team

Self-care is not "self-ish." It's smart living and smart business. True, there is no "I" in team, but there is a "me" when you turn things around and understand that when you prioritize your health and well-being, you are better equipped to impact the world around you. Don't let a faulty narrative prevent you from taking better care of yourself. When you care for you, the payoff is your ability to thrive in health and happiness for the best experience of life, both at home and at work.

Now, on the lines below, make a compelling *business case* for self-care. Don't merely rehash what you've heard. Articulate it for yourself in a compelling way that really captures and holds your attention.

_____

_____

_____

_____

_____

_____

_____

_____

_____

_____

WarriHER Wisdom on Well-Being

Although we can all probably agree that well-being involves health and happiness, it's when we get specific that well-being takes shape and provides real meaning to our own lives. Here's what warriHERs have to say about well-being. As you meet and hear from each warriHER, engage and interact with her by underlining or highlighting points with which you agree, by using an exclamation point (!) or (Yes) to signify points that really resonate with you, by using an (x) or (No) to signify points with which you disagree or which don't apply to you or your situation. Once you have met all ten warriHERs and have made notations along the way, your idea of what well-being means for you should have more clarity and depth for you.

WarriHER Wisdom on Well-Being
Baylie

To me, well-being means taking care of my body, my mind, and my soul. Taking care of my body means taking care of my health, such as exercising, paying attention to the foods I eat, and fueling it with the necessary vitamins it needs. Taking care of my mind can range from activities such as reading, listening to podcasts, partaking in different educational classes, meditating, etc. Taking care of my soul can mean making my home a place of comfort and allotting time for activities that truly relax me, such as praying, sitting in silence, and getting a massage.

Though I am an extrovert, my friends have quickly learned that I need to set time aside each week to be alone and decompress. It's a set commitment to myself in order to be the best me I can be. My co-workers have also learned that when I arrive in the morning, I need time to get my day started without being bombarded with stupid or non-stupid questions. They say "Hello" and then give me 10-15 minutes to catch up on email and mentally prepare myself for the day. In my 27 years, I've gotten to know myself pretty well. This makes prioritizing easier. I am aware of how I operate best, and I make the necessary adjustments to make myself the priority. In that way, I ensure that everyone with whom I interact gets the best version of me.

WarriHER Wisdom on Well-Being
Carrie

Well-being means that my entire being is well. It includes my body, spiritual connection, life experience including my relationships, and how I contribute value and receive value back (get paid!). All areas are equally important! I don't believe in balance—it's so delicate. If one thing doesn't go as planned (a.k.a. normal life), then everything is thrown off. Instead, I work toward harmony. When my being is in harmony, I am my best in all areas.

I used to prioritize work over everything else. Yes, work is important and making a great contribution to the world is a joy, but when work becomes the sole focus, a person loses effectiveness and joy. It took me a long time to realize this. I thought hours equals value. I did reach a great level of success, but I was chronically stressed, resentful, and joyless. It was not sustainable. Now, I make it my responsibility to keep my being in harmony so I can have an amazing life experience and be my best for my work, family, community… the world!

How do I prioritize self-care to stay in harmony? First, I'm really clear about what's important to me. The daily self-care items on my list are a sustainable morning routine, exercise every day, meditation twice a day, eating healthy, getting enough sleep, keeping my skin and hair well moisturized, reading before bed at night, and listening to music when I cook.

Second, I don't give myself too many choices. Part of making self-care work is being committed to it, which isn't always easy! I don't drink alcohol, I work out every day unless there is some totally impossible schedule issue, I limit my social media to be very intentional, and I don't watch TV other than family movie time a couple times a week. This isn't meant to say, "Yay me." It's the truth.

I take self-care and remaining in harmony seriously. It's my responsibility, and I have to recommit to it every day. Some days I don't feel like working out, but I still do it. And now I find joy every single day!

WarriHER Wisdom on Well-Being
ChrisTiana

Well-being can—and does—mean something different depending on the weather and terrain of my life journey in that moment. When skies are gray, I feel hip-deep in mud, or the trail seems impassable. Finding meaning and understanding through radical self-inquiry and deconstruction of harmful narratives has helped me illuminate a few beginning pathways to well-being and self-care.

As a non-binary, black and indigenous, multiple-disabled person, I will likely never truly be free of social constructs within my short lifetime. Our society has a very long road ahead in achieving social equity, collectivistic empathy, and lovingkindness. But what has soothed my soul, kept me grounded, and motivates me to continue this life journey every day is finding grounding in my understanding of what it means to exist—my purpose—and living my own construction of what it means to be "well." After all, every traveler needs a compass.

Since I can remember, I have been called "unwell" in some form. My severe asthma, frequent attacks, and hypersensitivity to allergies have led adults around me to treat me with—dare I say it?—kid gloves. As a young child, I began to learn what it meant to be regarded as "unwell," and the environment of my life journey was full of pathogens just waiting to kill me.

When I started elementary school, teachers and child psychologists told my mom that I had a developmental disability and I was "unwell." For 13 years, the diagnosis was re-storied as a "problem;" the way I traversed the path of my life journey would be incompatible with viable success since it was so different from the neurotypical movement of my peers.

In my early adulthood, I was involuntarily institutionalized in psychiatric asylums and hospitals for years. They told my family that I had developed a psychosis and I was "unwell." It took more than seven years to break free of a vortex that kept landing me back in the little room without a bra or shoelaces. They had coded me a threat to myself and sought to remove me from my life journey—or else hold me there shackled along the muddy shoulder of the path.

Through radical auto-ethnography and reflection, I have challenged a lifetime's worth of social conditioning to have me remain uncomfortably nestled in the trauma and anxiety of being relegated as the one who is "unwell." In this project of self-discovery and healing, I have found my well-being to be inextricably intertwined with deep, intrinsic meaning. What does it mean for others to deem me "unwell"? On what grounds is it based? By whose standards? And why? Most importantly, is the litmus test even agreeable to *my* understanding of well-being? So far, the answer to that question has continued to be a resounding NO. This is not to say that I have overcome anything internally.

There was never anything to internally overcome. But I have learned to live my life in harmony with my understanding of it, and that means taking an empathetically critical approach to society's attempts to story my life in a way that invalidates or suppresses the authorship of my own embodied narrative.

WarriHER Wisdom on Well-Being
Harriet

To me, well-being means prioritizing my needs—making them as important as the needs of others: family, work, etc.

It took some time for my family to get used to the idea that it's important for me to take care of myself. It wasn't so much my immediate family as my elderly parents and siblings. They have been so used to me putting their needs first (Yes, that was my fault) that it took them by surprise when I started to either say No or find other solutions to their priorities. It's still a constant struggle with them—it's a constant reminder.

WarriHER Wisdom on Well-Being
Jemia

Well-being equals self-care to me. Ensuring that my mind, body, and soul are taken care of in any- and everything that I do. Well-being doesn't just stop when I have completed my tasks or taken care of my family; it's how I live my life every day. I frequently hear the phrase "I have to take care of myself" when someone has a lot going on—which is understandable. However, that same mindset should be with us consistently. But I get it, and this is hard to do.

I try and prioritize my self-care each day. I look at my schedule for the day and think about when I am going to fit in time to enjoy something that brings me back to my center. It can be anything from taking a walk, listening to a podcast, and reading a chapter from a non-work-related book. My new favorite thing to do is to watch music videos from the 90s.

At first, I thought my self-care was to put my time and energy into my side hustle projects. Blogging, building up my social following, or conducting research. But that ended up contributing to my low energy levels even more. I had to start doing activities that allow my mind to drift away from whatever tasks are at hand.

Self-care is first. It should come before everything I do. If I'm not right with myself or love myself, how can I be whole for whatever comes my way?

WarriHER Wisdom on Well-Being
Laura

Well-being is a matter of holistically experiencing wellness. This means understanding the many dimensions of wellness and how they are interconnected—financially, emotionally, career-wise, sexually, spiritually, physically, environmentally, and socially. Finding true well-being means looking at all of these areas and observing where I am strong and where I need support.

I prioritize self-care because if I am not well, then I cannot support anyone or anything I love in return. A depleted professional, mom, friend, etc. can't do any role well. I have found time-blocking to be the most effective tool. I have clearly-set times for each thing I need to do, including things that refuel my tank. That means when it's time to work, I only work. But when it's time to be present with a book, or with friends over dinner, I don't let work or family life bleed into those spaces (as much as possible).

As women we are asked to be everything to everyone at all times. This leaves us doing nothing well and wondering what the point of all of this is anyway. Life is more than a series of tasks, and women don't need to apologize for prioritizing the things that bring us true joy—no matter what that looks like for each of us.

WarriHER Wisdom on Well-Being
Mayerland

Well-being is a comfort and peace within myself that I am good. I'm good with my life. I'm good with my health. I'm good in my faith. I'm good with what I believe the future holds for me, and I am doing what needs to be done to reach my goals.

It's very introspective. It's not about how others feel I am doing, but how I judge myself. I give myself permission to be good to me and to feel good about my decisions.

When I get out of balance, that is when I know some self-care is in order. Self-care is the action behind recognizing that if I do not take care of myself, I will be unable to take care of anyone or anything else.

I'm a Gen Xer. I have the work ethic of a Baby Boomer, but the work-life balance desires of Gen Y. I sacrificed my younger years, paid my dues for the reward of a very comfortable retirement in the future. Sacrifice has entailed working vacations, reduced sleep, and a constant connection to work email. I rationalized that it will pay off in the long run. It wasn't until I had a health scare that I realized that lack of sleep and constant stress can lead to some serious conditions that diet, exercise, and vitamin supplements can't fix.

I decided that eight hours of sleep each night, eight hours of meaningful family time per week, and semi-annual girls' weekends were non-negotiables! I also insist on keeping all of my maintenance appointments, which includes hair, mani/pedi, lash extensions, and massages as often as possible. I'm no longer saving the spa gift cards my work team gives me for that special occasion. I book those as soon as I get them. For context, all of my maintenance appointments are so much more effective when accompanied by a nice glass of wine.

WarriHER Wisdom on Well-Being
Nani

I used to think that as long as I got a clean bill of health at my annual physical and worked out regularly, I was considered "well." I was not a big athlete, but as a former dancer and a part-time fitness instructor in my 20's, I thought I could handle anything life threw at me. How narrow-minded it was to consider just my physical condition.

As my career and personal life became full and demanding in my 30's and 40's, I was finding less time to prioritize my health, both physically and emotionally. For decades, I drove myself hard with a demanding career that included extensive travel in addition to having and raising three children in the span of four and a half years.

I would like to think I was fulfilled and in a state of well-being, but the pressure to be the best in all areas of my life became overwhelming. I wasn't self-aware enough at the time to recognize how it was damaging my mental, physical and emotional state. I was driven by the notion of "doing it all," and achieving everything I set out to do, while completely ignoring my inner voice.

I placed my focus on what I thought I had to do, not wanting to let anyone down, especially myself. I wouldn't dare complain because, by all standards, I had a good life, but I couldn't explain why I was feeling empty, drained, and unhappy. I had so much to be thankful for, but there were major holes in my life that needed to be addressed.

By my mid 40's, I started to shed my false sense of fulfillment and learned to let go of the guilt. The journey was not an easy one, but I'm so grateful for the lessons that came with it. I have learned that self-care and self-love are mindful choices. I had to reassess my values and honor my internal voice.

Today, well-being for me means to be kind and gentle with myself, to listen to my body, mind, and soul and to align my choices with my authentic self. It's a practice of being self-aware and being present in the moment. I don't have to do it all, but whatever I do, I do it with heart. Simple choices, like taking a break to meditate or pray, going on walks in nature with my dog, dancing, hosting a casual dinner with friends, or getting a massage boosts my spirit.

I no longer feel guilty indulging myself. It requires being purposeful each day, writing down my intentions, carving out time for activities that bring me joy and create positive vibes. It's an ongoing practice to slow down and be fully present, just be—not always do. Searching for and living my purpose and calling. "Be still and know that I am God" (Psalms 46:10).

WarriHER Wisdom on Well-Being
Rhoda

Well-being to me means being in harmony within myself. It starts within me, having and maintaining balance within me. It's me having good health mentally, physically, and emotionally.

Well-being for me is when my spirit, soul, and body are aligned. This alignment starts from my spirit and transcends to my soul and then to my body, creating harmony. When harmony is not present, it's difficult to be healthy. When I think of health, for me it means mentally, emotionally, and physically healthy.

When I have this within me, I have peace that everything is as it should be and that I am on the right path. I am happy knowing no external circumstances can affect me unless I allow it. This also helps me to manage my expectations of people and of life. Both can be disappointing at times, but when I learn to manage my expectations, life becomes simpler.

When I prioritize self-care, I have no guilt. I always keep myself in the equation. I don't have a particular structure because my needs change from time to time. At times I need to focus more on my emotional needs, and at times I focus more on the physical. What's important is that I pay attention to me and my needs and factor them into my schedule.

I prioritize family, and I prioritize exercise four times a week. In addition, because I assign special priority to my spiritual health, I ensure I spend time meditating, praying, and studying the Bible. Doing this helps me with any challenges I face, gives me peace, and keeps me grounded.

I also make time to connect with my mentors. They are my sounding boards and help me navigate.

I must confess that I struggle with achieving work-life balance. I know it sounds strange, but because I love what I do, I am constantly working. I get ideas and concepts watching shows, speaking to people, and even when I'm resting.

My work is my destiny. I went through a difficult time with work. There were so many decisions to make, and I was depleted at the time. I had worked hard and pushed the whole year without taking a vacation. Needless to say, by December, I was spent, and I didn't want to continue with anything. I got to a point of feeling helplessness because I was exhausted and couldn't strategize for the following year

It took me six months to recover. Since then, I make sure I take a few days out of every month just to refuel. If I don't do this, my natural tendency toward my work would take over.

WarriHER Wisdom on Well-Being
Sara

To me, well-being means that my mind is at ease. It means I'm not ruminating on what I could have or should have done or said, and that I know in my heart and mind that I've done, and am doing, the best I can do in my work and in my relationships. As an autistic person, this has not come easily to me, and it's something I work on regularly—that is, to be satisfied with being me.

Although I didn't receive an autism diagnosis until I was 41, I knew there was something different about me throughout my life. I was quite terrified that there was something desperately wrong with me and was afraid to find out what it was. Although I held down jobs, had friends, and was married and had a child, I had a running dialogue in my mind that told me I was constantly making mistakes and saying and doing the wrong things. There were others in my life who were willing enough to support that opinion, pointing out my failings along with me. I now know this is a common theme for autistic people and for many women as well.

When I finally got up the courage at age 29 to seek therapy (for marriage counseling), the counselor was also willing to support the "there is something terribly wrong with you" opinion. It was devastating to me. So I left marriage counseling and, ultimately, the marriage. Then I went into individual counseling. It was there that I learned, through years of hard work, that my inner voice and the outer voices that wanted to put me down were wrong. I learned I was in fact highly compassionate, motivated, thoughtful, and kind. Just not to myself.

Once I learned about my autism diagnosis, things fell into place. I began the hard work of integrating the parts of my personality that had become splintered as a result of a childhood where pretty much everyone told me to be someone or act like someone that I simply wasn't—so that others could be happy.

Now, when I find myself under stress, I take a step back and remind myself who I am and what I believe. I'm careful to surround myself with people who are accepting and not rejecting, people who don't feel a need to fix me. My work also supports my well-being, because through it, I have the immense privilege of working with other autistic people so that they, too, can enjoy the satisfaction that comes with being oneself.

Battle Plan #3 Speaking of Well-Being

You can't address what you don't define or understand in detail. When you look back at your "interactions" with warriHERs, what themes and patterns emerge?

_____

_____

_____

_____

_____

_____

What and who contributes to your ability to thrive in life both personally and professionally?

_____

_____

_____

_____

_____

_____

_____

_____

Ready to put it all together? What is your definition of well-being in your own life? Draft your definition below. Be as in-depth or as succinct as you want to be. What's important is that you articulate a definition that has power for you.

_____

_____

_____

_____

_____

_____

_____

_____

_____

_____

_____

_____

_____

_____

_____

Now read out loud what you've written.

How does it sound? Is it convincing? Does it inspire you? Did you use your "I" voice? (I, me, my, myself, mine, etc.)

Try it again, and this time remove any references to "you" and write as if your (quality of) life were at stake.

_____

_____

_____

_____

_____

_____

_____

_____

_____

_____

_____

_____

_____

_____

What are the underlying differences between your two versions?

_____

_____

_____

_____

_____

What accounts for these differences?

_____

_____

_____

_____

_____

Though your definition of well-being is (and should be) unique to you, please consider these four underlying pillars of well-being.

- Purpose & Meaning

- Physical Wellness

- Belonging

- Fun

These four pillars make up what I call the Circle of Well-Being.

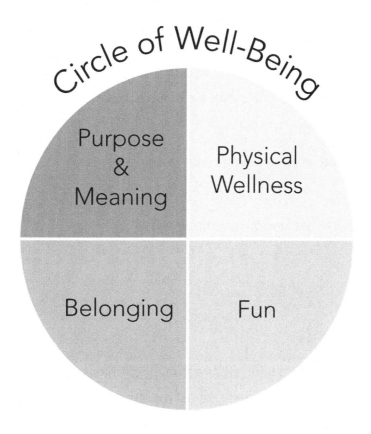

Battle Plan #4 You're Being Audited!

Well-Being Audit (Phase 1)

How much <u>importance</u> do you give each of the following? Circle your rating. A rating of 10 means maximum importance; a rating of 0 means no importance.

Having a clear and strong sense of purpose and meaning in my life:

0   1   2   3   4   5   6   7   8   9   10

Eating, exercising, hydrating, and sleeping in ways that support my body and mind:

0   1   2   3   4   5   6   7   8   9   10

Maintaining close relationships at work and outside of work:

0   1   2   3   4   5   6   7   8   9   10

Engaging in behaviors that bring me enjoyment:

0   1   2   3   4   5   6   7   8   9   10

Well-Being Audit (Phase 2)

Over the past six months to a year, what actual <u>effort</u> have you devoted to each of the following? Circle your rating. A rating of 10 means maximum effort; a rating of zero means no effort.

Having a clear and strong sense of purpose and meaning in my life:

0   1   2   3   4   5   6   7   8   9   10

Eating, exercising, hydrating, and sleeping in ways that support my body and mind:

0   1   2   3   4   5   6   7   8   9   10

Maintaining close relationships at work and outside of work:

0   1   2   3   4   5   6   7   8   9   10

Engaging in behaviors that bring me enjoyment:

0   1   2   3   4   5   6   7   8   9   10

There are four key supporting players of all four pillars of the Circle of Well-Being. They include:

- intimacy with a partner

- a safe environment

- career satisfaction

- adequate finances

Review your completed well-being audits. Consider what gaps exist between what you say and what you model. The greater the gap, the greater the probability of a disconnect that will continue to threaten your overall well-being.

For reference, among the four factors in the audit, place a check (√) beside your highest scoring factor in Phase 1 and also place a check (√) beside your highest scoring factor in Phase 2.

Now place an (x) beside your lowest scoring factors in Phase 1 and in Phase 2. What patterns and trends emerge? What conclusions can you draw? Record your thoughts.

_____

_____

_____

_____

_____

_____

_____

_____

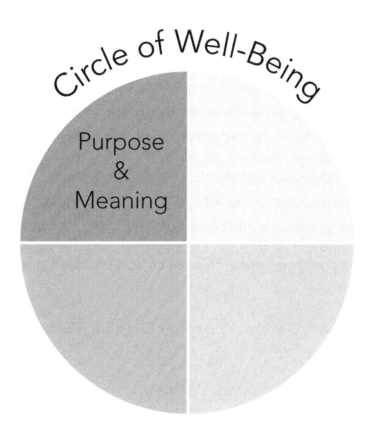

Circle of Well-Being

Purpose
&
Meaning

Battle Plan #5 Cranking up the Stillness

One minute. That's all. That's the length of time I give participants to close or lower their eyes, clear their minds, and focus on their breathing. It's the same amount of time I'll give you.

Great power and wisdom can come from stillness, especially when it involves matters of purpose and meaning. Slowing down to practice the art of stillness remains among the hardest things to do for busy, performance-driven people.

Find a quiet place that evokes a sense of calm with you. Use a timer with an audible alarm. If during the one minute, you feel your mind drifting, gently bring your focus back to your breathing. Also, try and block out any visual or auditory stimulus.

Set the timer for one minute, and with eyes closed or lowered, begin. Now reflect back on your experience.

How did you feel? Relaxed? Tense? What else? Describe your feelings here.

_____

_____

_____

_____

Did you fidget or stay still? Describe your body movements.

_____

_____

_____

_____

Did your mind drift off and get cynical? ("This is stupid." "This is a waste of time.")

_____

_____

_____

_____

_____

Did one minute feel too short, just right, or too long? Elaborate.

_____

_____

_____

_____

_____

What would be the value to you of practicing stillness?

_____

_____

_____

_____

This busy, technologically-saturated age in which we live has trained us to attend to and do many things at once. Our minds are constantly cranked up while our spirits are turned down. Some of us may have forgotten how to be alone with ourselves or to listen to silence.

Among the benefits of mindful stillness is that it sets the stage for us to become more attuned to purpose and meaning. I invite you to turn down the "noise" and crank up your mind and spirit as you begin the journey to exploring your purpose.

Battle Plan #6 Dis-Covering You on Purpose

"What is my purpose?

"What am I supposed to be doing?"

If you are constantly asking yourself these questions, then perhaps what you're doing is not it. Some people confuse their job (vocation) with their purpose. The two are not necessarily one and the same. It's great when you can discover alignment between your job and your purpose. Purpose is the "secret sauce" of our life that gives us staying power by providing us with passion and resilience.

Purpose helps us to have better insight into an appropriate job or role menu. It is where your natural gifts and talents intersect with difference-making. I'm making a distinction between natural gifts and talents on the one hand and skill on the other for a reason. You can learn a skill and be really good at it, but your natural gifts and talents are inherently wired. When you are activated to utilize your natural wiring, you get a far deeper fulfillment and satisfaction than whatever beneficial results emerge from a skill you've mastered.

While skills can be lost if they are not practiced and used often, natural gifts and talents are a part of who you are, and you never lose them for as long as you have breath. Yes, your gifts and talents will go through various stages of maturity and expression, but they will always remain your gifts and talents. And when you use them in service of something beyond yourself to make a difference in the lives of others, you are expressing and living in your purpose.

The best shorthand for purpose that I've ever heard is this: "When I use my gifts and talents to make a difference, that's when I feel the most alive." Living with purpose makes the difference between surviving and thriving. The journey of discovering your purpose can be one of the most fulfilling journeys you'll experience in your lifetime.

Are you ready to begin yours?

In response to each of these questions, free flow your thoughts and write them down without self-editing along the way. Don't worry about getting it just right or about complete sentences. Capture the sentiment without regard for form or fashion. The questions are deliberately broad for maximum freedom. If your first reaction is to question the question, you are not yet ready to begin the journey. If that's the case, take a break and come back to the questions when you feel more uninhibited and receptive.

What did I like doing before time, money, and responsibilities got in the way?

_____

_____

_____

_____

_____

_____

What do I like doing now?

_____

_____

_____

_____

_____

_____

What am I good at?

_____

_____

_____

_____

_____

_____

_____

What do others say I'm good at?

_____

_____

_____

_____

_____

_____

_____

What is important to me?

Battle Plan #7 Mapping Your Purpose DNA

For most people, purpose is connected to one or more of the following five outcomes. Read through the list below, let yourself savor them, and say each one out loud. Pay attention to your visceral responses. Because purpose is a driving force that resonates deeply, notice if every cell of your body activates for any of the elements, if you get goosebumps, or if the hair on the back of your neck stands up.

Circle the one that you resonate with the most. Whichever one draws you in and pulls you in the most is a big clue that will help you to get more purpose-specific. If none of these resonates with you, devote some additional time to thinking through what's missing from the list for you. Then formulate a general element of your own.

- making a difference

- being of service to others

- leaving a legacy

- achieving happiness/fulfillment

- being extraordinary in role(s)

Does what you've selected surprise you? Why or why not? Record your thoughts.

_____

_____

_____

_____

_____

_____

Battle Plan #8 Connecting to Your Values

Review the values below and circle the 10 values that are the most important to you.

balance	family	integrity
character	freedom	kindness
commitment	generosity	security
compassion	growth	loyalty
responsibility	authenticity	openness
courage	happiness	optimism
creativity	harmony	perseverance
excellence	knowledge/wisdom	health
faith	respect	trust
fairness	humor	service

From the 10 values you circled above, select your top 5 and list them in priority order.

#1 _____

#2 _____

#3 _____

#4 _____

#5 _____

What, if anything, surprises you about your top five values? Why?

_____

_____

_____

_____

_____

_____

_____

_____

How do your top five values show up in your work?

_____

_____

_____

_____

_____

_____

_____

Battle Plan #9 Walking the Right Talk

Consider the following 10 behaviors and traits that support well-being. Place a check (√) next to each that has consistently characterized you over the past six months to a year.

_____ 1. I acknowledge that I cannot control all circumstances in life.

_____ 2. I carve out time for honest and introspective looks at my life.

_____ 3. I simplify and de-clutter my life.

_____ 4. I take care of myself.

_____ 5. I slow down, enjoy life, laugh more, and worry less.

_____ 6. I connect meaningfully with those I care about.

_____ 7. I free myself from the self-imposed pressure to be perfect.

_____ 8. I appreciate the beauty in my surroundings.

_____ 9. I make choices that are aligned with my values.

_____ 10. I seize moments to just "be."

Record the total number of checks (√) _____.

Understanding your results:

8 to 10 checked—You exhibit healthy and positive behaviors that lend themselves to optimal well-being.

6 to 7 checked—You are limited and bound by behaviors that negatively affect your capacity for optimal well-being.

3 to 5 checked—You are prone to stress and catastrophizing, which severely restricts your capacity for optimal well-being.

0 to 2 checked—You operate in survival mode, which, if not addressed, may ultimately result in burnout.

What are your take-aways from this exercise? Record your thoughts.

_____

_____

_____

_____

_____

_____

_____

_____

_____

_____

_____

_____

_____

_____

_____

_____

_____

Battle Plan #10 Identifying Heroes

Each of us, no doubt, has at least one person who has deeply impacted our life in a profound and meaningful way—shaping who we are and, perhaps, even changing our life's entire trajectory. My life's purpose reflects individuals who sowed meaning into my life. Experience has taught me three important things: that it is impossible to impact others without being impacted ourselves; that what we do for others, we do for ourselves; that what we "give away," we receive.

Devote some time to remind yourself of a person(s) of lasting impact and to remind yourself that you, too, are a person of lasting impact with endless opportunities to impact others.

Write down three people who have had a tremendously positive impact on your life or who have accomplished something that you would like to do. Because of them, toward what purpose or cause might you want to devote yourself?

Name of person	What the person did	What I might do

Name three people for whom you have had a tremendous positive impact on their lives.

Name of person	The impact I have made on this person's life

What have you discovered or rediscovered about yourself from this exercise?

_____

_____

_____

_____

_____

Battle Plan #11 Designing Your Own Rules

Here's a question that is also well worth pondering: *Where do your happiness and fulfillment come from?* Do you think you get them from chasing accomplishment, achievement, and accumulation? If so, were there times when you didn't get that result? What was going on in your life then? Who was in your life then? Do you suppose that what you were really chasing was within you—not outside of you?

Over the years, I have listened to and read quite a lot about the distinctions between happiness and fulfillment/meaning. The field of positive psychology has provided a plethora of knowledge and an abundance of happiness experts. But why should you let the experts make the rules regarding your happiness and fulfillment? You are probably not a psychologist (nor am I), but you are the happiness and fulfillment expert of your own life. Do you really want to know whose concept of happiness and fulfillment really counts? Yours. How you conceive of happiness and fulfillment operating in your life can shape how effectively you navigate your life.

You are more empowered than you even realize to create and assign meaning—and that is good news. Happiness and fulfillment for you are what you say they are for you. Happiness and fulfillment for me are what I say they are for me.

Design your own rules. Design your life. Create your own paradigms.

To guide and prepare you for shaping your own paradigms of happiness and fulfillment, I offer you mine as a reference point:

Happiness

Happiness for me is a feel-good feeling that can be fleeting. It's elusive. It ebbs and flows with whatever circumstances, small or otherwise, are happening in my life. Happiness comes from "happenings." When good things happen, I am happy. When bad things happen, I am usually unhappy. My happiness can be influenced by things I both can and cannot control. I feel happy when I am planning my perfect vacation. I may not be so happy if it rains the entire time. I feel happy when I get upgraded to a first-class seat on my flight. I am not so happy when I am relegated to a middle seat.

Sometimes my happiness depends on the happiness of others. And I have been reminded several times how my happiness (or lack thereof) impacts others. If you ask him, my husband will assure you, without hesitation, that in our family "if I ain't happy, ain't nobody happy!" My happiness and unhappiness show up on my face.

Your Notes/Observations: _____

_____

_____

_____

_____

_____

_____

Fulfillment

I view fulfillment as a deep sense of inner satisfaction. In my own life, it is a steady peace, a state of equilibrium and well-being that live in my spirit. It is not dependent on any outside circumstances. Because fulfillment is tied to my deeper purpose, I can be experiencing an unhappy moment but still maintain a sense of fulfillment. Fulfillment gives me the strength and fortitude to persevere through periods of trial. Unlike happiness that can come and go, fulfillment takes up permanent residence inside of me. Fulfillment lodges deep within me and becomes my center, my source, and my anchor to get me back on track if/when I allow my life to go off track. My fulfillment grows and flourishes when I am consistently operating from my passion and feeding into others. Fulfillment is knowing that I live and operate in true alignment. Starkly different from the fleeting vapor that happiness is, fulfillment sustains me and gives me staying power for the long-term. While happiness only shows up on my face, fulfillment also emanates from my spirit.

Your Notes/Observations:

_____

_____

_____

_____

_____

_____

How about you? How do you conceive of happiness for *you*?

_____

_____

_____

_____

_____

_____

_____

_____

_____

How do conceive of fulfillment for *you*?

_____

_____

_____

_____

_____

_____

_____

_____

Battle Plan #12 Re-Make this Job and Love It

Typically, when people say they don't have work-life balance, we intuitively know what that doesn't mean. For example, Jackie isn't saying that she is giving way too much of herself to family members and friends. Nor is Karen saying that she is spending way too much energy on hobbies. And Cathy isn't saying she devotes way too much of herself to self-care. A lack of work-life balance always refers to how much of yourself you give to work to the detriment of all other aspects of your life.

Loved ones often classify work as the enemy. But work is not the real enemy. Work has a very practical purpose. Work can allow you to exercise your gifts, talents, and skills in the noble service of something greater than yourself. Work can give you an outlet and expression for your creativity and your passions. Work allows you to provide a living for yourself and also provide for those who are dependent upon you. Work allows you to provide for needs and even indulge your wants.

Asking tough questions about work helps you make decisions about how best to integrate work into your life so that it does not overshadow everything else.

Are you ready to evaluate what work means to you?

As you consider the following questions, be open to recording your raw, blunt truth. Exhaust each question until you can write no more. Only then will you have treated each question with the appropriate level of depth. When you believe that you have exhausted your response to a question, pause to read your response out loud to yourself so that you can hear how it sounds. If necessary, add to what you have written. Do this several times until you are finally sure that you have exhausted the question. Then you will be ready to proceed to the next question. Repeat this entire process with each successive question.

1.   Do you find your current work enjoyable? Why or why not?

_____

_____

_____

_____

_____

_____

_____

2.   What are some things you can do that are within your control to make work enjoyable or even more enjoyable?

_____

_____

_____

_____

_____

_____

_____

3.   What do you like most about your work? How much time do you devote to these aspects of your work? How can you shift more time to them?

_____

_____

_____

_____

_____

_____

_____

_____

4.   What do you like least about your work? How much time do you devote to them? How can you shift less time to these aspects of your work?

_____

_____

_____

_____

_____

_____

_____

5.   How would you characterize or describe your perfect job? What makes it perfect?

_____

_____

_____

_____

_____

_____

_____

_____

6.   How important is it for you to feel passionate about your work? Do you?

_____

_____

_____

_____

_____

_____

_____

_____

7. What do you do during your entire day (from the time you wake until the time you retire for the night) that you feel most passionate about?

_____

_____

_____

_____

_____

_____

_____

Based on your responses, what adjustments would you want or need to make concerning your work in order to love it? Are these adjustments do-able and practical for your situation? What support—and whose—would you need to enlist to make those changes?

_____

_____

_____

_____

_____

_____

Battle Plan #13 Ditching Work-Life Balance for Work-Life Fit

"I don't have work-life balance. I want it. I need it."

I hear this all the time from workshop participants and new coaching clients. My response usually takes people by surprise: "Have you defined what work-life balance would look like, sound like, and feel like for you and your situation?"

After a moment of silence, the answer I get is almost always "No," accompanied by downcast eyes. But how can we say we want something when we have not determined what that something is? In light of that, here are a few questions for you:

What is your definition of work-life balance (or work-life integration, work-life harmony, or whatever terms you use to characterize an optimal blending of your professional and personal life)?

_____

_____

_____

_____

_____

_____

_____

_____

_____

Based on your definition, do you currently have work-life balance? Circle your answer.

YES   NO

If Yes, explain how you came to have it. If No, explain why you don't have it.

_____

_____

_____

_____

_____

_____

Do you think it's possible for you to have work-life balance? Circle your answer.

YES   NO

First, the good news. If you answered "Yes," you are right. It is possible for you to have work-life balance.

Here's the not-so-good news. If you answered "No," you are right. It is not possible for you to have work-life balance.

Do you see where this is going? Your ability to have balance (or not) is within your control, but you must first set your mind on what you want. When you define your work-life balance, you give yourself a target toward which to direct your efforts.

I like to use the term work-life "fit" because it is your definition—customized and tailored to fit you—based on what and who is important to you. It is yours and yours alone, so it suits you! Did you catch that? It fits YOU.

Let's go deeper using four steps: acknowledge your responsibility, create a declaration of truth, create a visualization, and make your "fit" adaptable.

Acknowledgment

As a starting point, it's important to acknowledge that you are responsible for your life. If you don't have work-life balance, after all, who do you think is ultimately responsible? Yes: *you*. Not your manager, not your HR department, not your [complete with whatever or whomever you wish to blame]. Maybe you need to admit that you didn't adequately strategize and execute on ensuring a better work-life fit for yourself. Who didn't? You. That's powerful.

I readily acknowledge that I:

_____

_____

_____

_____

_____

_____

_____

Read your acknowledgment out loud to yourself several times. Now, in front of a mirror, make eye contact with your mirror image and speak your acknowledgment without looking at what you have written. Now, enlist your partner or other trusted loved one and verbally acknowledge what you have acknowledged to yourself.

Declaration

The second step is to begin to embody the power you already have, but haven't yet tapped into, to achieve a better work-life fit. It's your Declaration of Truth. Mine was this:

There is not a person, job, company, system, or process on this earth that can keep me away from what I most value and care about!

Think about a forceful declaration or mantra that empowers you to take back control of your life and that you can repeat to yourself during moments when extra motivation and a fighting spirit are needed. Ideally, your declaration should be a single sentence that you can easily memorize. Once you write it down, practice saying it to yourself and saying it out loud with power, boldness, and conviction.

_____

_____

_____

_____

_____

_____

Visualization

The third step is to create a visualization that inspires you. My visual involved the image of my right hand taking back the power and control I'd given away by blaming others for my failure to establish a better work-life balance for myself. I see myself extending my right hand away from me, snatching back my life with a closed fist, and pulling my fist back toward me.

According to the often-quoted writer of inspirational ideas, William Arthur Ward, "If you can imagine it, you can achieve it. If you can dream it, you can become it." This is the part where you get to create a scenario that allows you to recapture what has been lost. What you visualize and how it plays out can be as ordinary or incredible or fantastical as you like. What matters most is the outcome—gaining that which you seek. In other words, visualize yourself winning! For me, it was very important that the symbolism of mighty right-hand power and strength play a prominent role in reclaiming my life.

In your visualization, are you a giant? Do you have super-powers? Do you go up against a force or a person? Do you embark on a quest to find your "lost treasure" that has been trapped in a cave? Write out your visualization here, capturing any details that help make the visualization as real as possible. Once you have written it down and read it several times, close your eyes, breathe deeply, and let yourself enter the world of your visualization. Do it over and over again.

_____

_____

_____

_____

_____

_____

_____

_____

_____

_____

Adaptability

The final step is to clarify and refine your definition as needed. Based on the life choices you have made and practical considerations of your responsibilities and obligations, financial and otherwise, does your definition reflect a realistic fit for your circumstances? Does your definition only incorporate elements over which you have control?

After carefully reviewing your initial definition and giving further thought to practical considerations, write the latest iteration of your definition of work-life fit.

_____

_____

_____

_____

_____

_____

_____

_____

_____

_____

_____

_____

Battle Plan #14 Maintaining a Good Fit

We have to be realistic and recognize that circumstances change, needs change, and situations arise. For this reason, it is always a good idea to frequently evaluate and re-evaluate whether your current definition of work-life fit is still working for you. Is it organic and flexible enough to allow you to get back on track when you mess up or when circumstances beyond your control happen? And yes, even with the best definition and the best strategy, you may at times need to adapt.

Based on what you know of your life, what are some possible situations that might arise for which you can plan in advance? List them and start to sketch out a general plan of action you can take to adapt so that your sense of well-being doesn't get derailed.

"Disrupting" situation	General plan of action

Battle Plan #15 Valuing Fit

Based on how I've defined my own work-life fit, certain values emerge for me, including faith, family, friends, fitness, and fun—all of which I need to experience regularly for balance and well-being. Here's what that means for me:

If, on a given day, I experience aspects of all five, it's a great day. If I experience all aspects nearly every day, it's a great life. Even on a day when I experience only a single aspect, it's still an okay day. Because I've identified and articulated what I want to experience, I can track and assess how I'm doing and adjust as needed.

What about you? Based on your definition of work-life fit, what emerges for you? Review and circle (or write in your own) your top 10 you'd *like* to experience regularly.

family time	community service	laughter/humor
fun/leisure	faith practice	exercise/physical activity
purpose	love/intimacy	friendship/connection
television/movies	personal travel	reading
meditation	journaling	rest/relaxation
nature	learning	alone time
social media	hobbies	achievement
_____	_____	_____
_____	_____	_____
_____	_____	_____

From the 10 you identified above, select your top 5 you'd *NEED* to experience regularly in order to feel content and fulfilled. Write them in priority order below.

TOP 5 FOCUS AREAS

#1 _____

#2 _____

#3 _____

#4 _____

#5 _____

What, if anything, surprises you about your top five? What is the impact of seeing them listed? Record your thoughts.

_____

_____

_____

_____

_____

_____

_____

Now plan for your five priority focus areas by brainstorming some corresponding activities/behaviors about which you can be more deliberate.

FOCUS AREA	CORRESPONDING ACTIVITIES/BEHAVIORS

Battle Plan #16 Detoxing from Technology

When I facilitate group sessions, sometimes I like to stimulate dialogue around tough topics concerning the impact of work on home life. One question I pose is this: "What would you say is the biggest barrier for you in your relationships outside of work?" More times than not, people raise their smartphones in the air with one hand without saying a word. Sometimes, there are even a few participants in the room who have two smartphones, so they hold up one in one hand and one in the other.

What about you? Are you ever without your smartphone at arm's length? Is the thought of going 5, 10, 15 minutes without stealing a glance at your smartphone unthinkable? Are you currently involved in a co-dependent relationship with your smartphone? If you answered "Yes" to any of those questions, it may be time to disrupt your smartphone addiction.

Smartphones come equipped with a plethora of functions: email, text, apps, music, video, camera, and more. My unofficial research into smartphone usage revealed this not-so-surprising conclusion: The "talk on the phone" function is the least-used function on the devices.

For working professionals, it is typically the email function that can be the most challenging to self-regulate, which makes it a good starting place to examine your habits and begin to set boundaries that align with your well-being. The idea is to manage your smartphone so that your smartphone doesn't manage you.

What follows are ten ideas regarding establishing smartphone boundaries. Place a check (√) beside those to which you could commit.

_____ Remove work email account(s) from your smartphone.

_____ If you have two smartphones, dedicate one for work use and one for personal use.

_____ No smartphone use during mealtimes—whether alone or with others.

_____ No smartphone use or charging in the bedroom   .

_____ Program in your smartphone "Do Not Disturb" times.

_____ Set alerts with reminders to take a break from your smartphone.

_____ Stash your smartphone in a drawer and out of sight during meetings.

_____ Avoid checking your smartphone first thing in the morning when you wake up.

_____ Avoid checking your smartphone last thing at night before turning in.

How would you describe responsible smartphone usage for *you*?

_____

_____

_____

_____

_____

Jot down one idea to adjust/reduce your use of these:

Twitter: _____

FaceTime: _____

Instagram: _____

Games: _____

Other: _____

What one thing will you do differently from now on to detox from technology?

_____

_____

_____

Battle Plan #17 Putting You First

If going from putting yourself last to putting yourself first does not come easy, try this daily accountability check-in with yourself. By committing to and writing down a plan, you reinforce making yourself a priority and reflecting on the outcome.

WEEK OF _____

	INTENT One thing I will do today just for me.	ACTUAL OUTCOME One thing I did today just for me.
Sun		
Mon		
Tues		
Wed		
Thurs		
Fri		
Sat		

Battle Plan #18 Knowing Who You Are

Whether you realize it or not, deep reflection and introspection feed you. When they go missing for a while, a part of you is starving, whether you realize it or not. Kim was one of those busy people who believed that reflection, mindfulness, journaling, and even yoga were a waste of time. She equated her busy-ness with success. She believed her hyper-activity was evidence of her importance and that pursuits that didn't produce tangible, measurable results were best left to lazy and unambitious people.

One day Kim showed up in my Relationship Management Skills course because her manager felt she needed to work on her relationship skills with her direct reports.

During most of the session, Kim hemmed, hawed, and complained—except when she was on her smartphone. Flagrantly unengaged with the course content, she sat in the front of the room, a place where she seemed to be the most accustomed to assuming.

I could tell that she was going through the motions just so she could check the box attesting to her successful course completion. She wasn't concerned with being present, just attendance—not with learning, just credit. At one point during the afternoon portion, I assigned a writing assignment to everyone in the room. They were to write a response to the question, "Who are you?" until I called "Stop."

As everyone huddled down to begin the process, Kim sat there and glared at me with her arms folded. She looked around the room at what she thought were people being successful at something that she wasn't doing. If she had looked more closely, she would have noticed that there were also people in the room who were struggling, but unlike her, they were making an effort. It was an activity that was designed to awaken and provoke.

I deliberately gave Kim a few moments to squirm and grow more uncomfortable. I gave her time to let her guard down. I watched her grow small. Only then did I feel that the time was right; she would be humble enough and receptive enough to let me in.

I walked over to her and crouched down beside her to meet her at eye level.

"How can I help?" I asked.

In a small child-like whisper, she answered with, "I don't understand what I'm supposed to be doing."

With gentle firmness, I repeated the assignment, purposely not supplying her with more information, while intent on not letting her off the hook.

"You are to write a response to 'Who are you?'"

"But what do you mean by that?"

"What I mean by that is 'who are you?'"

"But I…it's just that…it seems like such…"

With no further warning, Kim burst into sobs. Between sobs, she managed to get out the following words: "But. [sob] I. Don't. [sob] Know. Who. I. Am. [sob sob]"

By then, everyone in the room was watching. I walked with her out of the room and into the hall. Thus began my working relationship with Kim.

In time, Kim would grow to be a huge proponent of reflection and, yes, journaling. She has shared many of her a-ha's with me. Today one of Kim's favorite topics to journal on is—yes, you guessed it—"Who are you?"

Perhaps, you can relate to Kim's starting point. Perhaps there is a bit of Kim in you. Access your "inner Kim" and respond to the question: "Who are you?" It may help to know that this particular question is *designed* to stretch you and cause discomfort—some level of struggle is expected. Take a deep breath and write and write and write. You will intuitively know when you are done.

_____

_____

_____

_____

_____

_____

_____

_____

Battle Plan #19 Trading Work for Purpose

All of the Battle Plans you've read so far lead to this one: trading work for purpose.

First, let's clarify what purpose is. Purpose is about transformation and how you impact others and the world. It is more than a recitation of your job description at work or the tasks you complete there. It is about having a calling to which you are deeply committed and for which you are uniquely already equipped.

I want to share mine with you in the hopes that you will be inspired to not only ignite your purpose but to articulate it in a way that activates every single cell in your body, gives you a case of full-body goosebumps, and makes the hair on the back of your neck stand at attention.

> *To serve and glorify God by planting a seed and ministering to the heart of each person He places in my path; to be used as a tool by Him to transform others and yet myself be transformed; to grow more Christ-like in my thoughts, words, and actions; to hear at the end of days, "Well done, good and faithful servant."*

Without a purpose, you have nowhere to go, nothing toward which to direct your energy. Before you begin to articulate a compelling purpose for yourself, consider that your true purpose will distinguish itself for you through its clarity, intensity, and depth. You will naturally give yourself over to your true purpose with wholeheartedness.

What is your purpose?

_____

_____

_____

_____

_____

Read it out loud to yourself. How do you feel?

_____

_____

_____

_____

_____

_____

_____

Read it out loud to someone you deeply love and trust. How do you feel?

_____

_____

_____

_____

_____

_____

_____

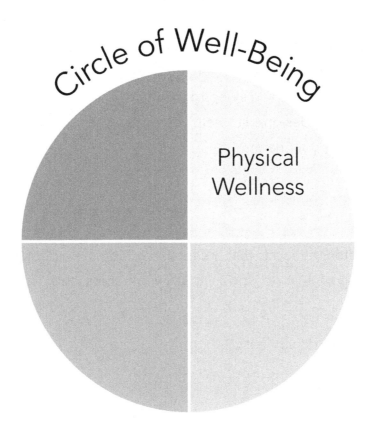

Circle of Well-Being

Physical
Wellness

Battle Plan #20 Eating on Purpose

Like me, you may not be a dietitian, nutritionist, or exercise physiologist. But you don't need to be an expert to understand the basics of physical wellness. Admit it. You already know on a basic level what you should and should not be doing from a wellness standpoint. You probably also know what you should and should not be doing about nutrition, exercise, hydration, and sleep to maintain your physical wellness.

This Battle Plan is designed to help you review some fundamentals of nutrition and to have you assess your habits.

Nutrition

Eat light and eat often the foods that are relatively high in nutrients and relatively low in calories, including protein-rich foods, fruits, vegetables, and grains.

On average, how often do you eat?

_____

_____

_____

Is that okay with you? Why or why not?

_____

_____

_____

_____

_____

What does it mean to you to eat often?

_____

_____

_____

What is the longest amount of time you've ever gone without eating?

_____

_____

Describe the circumstances that caused you to go without eating.

_____

_____

What does it mean to you to eat light?

_____

_____

Do you eat light? Why or why not?

_____

_____

_____

_____

Do you want to eat light? Why or why not?

_____

_____

_____

What percentage of the time do your meals include foods from at least one of these four categories: protein-rich foods, fruits, vegetables, and grains?

_____

_____

_____

What percentage of the time do you _want_ your meals to include foods from at least one of these four categories? Remember that this is not about perfection. It's about progress.

_____

_____

How do your current nutrition habits affect your ability to live out your purpose?

_____

_____

_____

_____

_____

Nutrition fuels the body, while purpose fuels the spirit. Based on your own understanding of the mind-body-spirit connection, what are some ideas for aligning your nutrition with your purpose?

Battle Plan #21 Designing Meals

In this Battle Plan, you'll list foods from each of the four categories that you'd enjoy eating as part of the following meals. Design meals that are practical for you and your situation. The idea is to keep prioritizing how you fuel your body and to keep honoring the important role that nutrition plays in your health and overall well-being.

Breakfast at Home	
protein-rich foods	
fruits	
vegetables	
grains	

Breakfast at Work	
protein-rich foods	
fruits	
vegetables	
grains	

Breakfast at the Airport	
protein-rich foods	
fruits	
vegetables	
grains	

Breakfast at a Fast-Food Establishment	
protein-rich foods	
fruits	
vegetables	
grains	

Breakfast at a Restaurant	
protein-rich foods	
fruits	
vegetables	
grains	

Lunch at Home	
protein-rich foods	
fruits	
vegetables	
grains	

Lunch at Work	
protein-rich foods	
fruits	
vegetables	
grains	

Lunch at Airport	
protein-rich foods	
fruits	
vegetables	
grains	

Lunch at a Fast-Food Establishment	
protein-rich foods	
fruits	
vegetables	
grains	

Lunch at a Restaurant	
protein-rich foods	
fruits	
vegetables	
grains	

Dinner at Home	
protein-rich foods	
fruits	
vegetables	
grains	

Dinner at the Airport	
protein-rich foods	
fruits	
vegetables	
grains	

Dinner at a Fast-Food Restaurant	
protein-rich foods	
fruits	
vegetables	
grains	

Dinner at a Restaurant	
protein-rich foods	
fruits	
vegetables	
grains	

Battle Plan #22 Exercising on Purpose

This Battle Plan will help you assess your exercise habits. According to Merriam Webster's Dictionary, exercise is the "regular or repeated use of a faculty or bodily organ for the sake of developing and maintaining physical fitness." According to the Oxford Dictionary, exercise is "activity requiring physical effort, carried out to sustain or improve health and fitness."

While the nuances of the definitions may vary, exercise is integral to our health and fitness. And as such, it is also key to overall well-being.

There are those who don't engage in exercise, and they have a variety of reasons for not doing so. Part of the key is to create a compelling reason to exercise and then build in support and accountability.

First, what is your definition of exercise?

_____

_____

_____

_____

Is exercise important to you? Why or why not?

_____

_____

_____

_____

_____

On average how often do you exercise during the week?

_____

Is that okay with you? Why or why not?

_____

_____

_____

What types of exercise do you engage in?

_____

_____

_____

_____

What types of exercises could you start doing that you would enjoy and consider fun? Expand your thinking and include activities that count as exercise.

_____

_____

_____

_____

_____

Use the fun activities you listed and provide detail in the charts.

Exercise Type—What activity will you be doing? (i.e., biking, yoga, volleyball, etc.)

Frequency—How often can you engage in this activity? (i.e., once a week on Saturday)

Duration—How much time can you carve out for this activity? (i.e., 30 minutes)

Setting—Where will you engage in this activity? (i.e., gym, park, office fitness center, etc.)

Buddy— Who will you enlist to join you? (i.e., partner, friend, colleague, etc.)

Tracking System—What method of accountability will you use? (i.e., Fitbit, app tracker, accountability buddy, etc.)

Exercise Type	
Frequency	
Duration	
Setting	
Buddy	
Tracking System	

Exercise Type	
Frequency	
Duration	
Setting	
Buddy	
Tracking System	

What is stopping you from implementing any of what you've described?

_____

_____

_____

_____

What steps can you take to implement what you've described?

_____

_____

_____

_____

Battle Plan #23 Hydrating on Purpose

The purpose of this Battle Plan is for you to assess your hydration habits throughout the day. There are some of us that are familiar with the "Drink 8-10 glasses of water a day" rule or the "Drink half your body weight of water in ounces" rule. No matter which one you subscribe to, it's advisable to ensure you're sufficiently hydrating throughout the day.

When and how much water, on average, do you drink daily?

_____

_____

_____

_____

_____

Are you okay with that? Why or why not?

_____

_____

_____

_____

_____

List the beverages you consume on a *regular* basis along with how much and how frequently.

beverage	amount	frequency

Consider the following strategies that are designed to increase hydration and prevent dehydration. Circle each strategy that you'd classify as do-able for you.

- Order only water with your food when dining out

- Opt for sparkling, zero-calorie water

- Keep a water bottle with you pre-filled with your daily allowance of water and sip it throughout the day until it is depleted

- Make a pitcher of fruit or vegetable-infused water for home consumption (i.e., strawberry, lemon, cucumber, etc.)

- Experiment with room-temperature or ice-cold water to determine preference

- Elevate your experience by drinking water from a wine glass at home

- Try "water on the rocks" with a paper straw

- Engage in exercise and strenuous activity to drive thirst

- Drink unsweetened tea

What additional strategies can you list? Record them here.

_____

_____

_____

_____

_____

Keeping in mind a connection with your purpose, how will you benefit from adequate water intake?

_____

_____

_____

_____

Outline a general plan of action to optimize your water intake.

_____

_____

_____

_____

_____

_____

_____

_____

_____

_____

_____

_____

_____

_____

_____

_____

_____

_____

Battle Plan #24 Sleeping on Purpose

The purpose of this Battle Plan is for you to assess your sleep habits. Sleeping seven to eight hours per night has long been considered the golden rule. Only elite athletes and select others with a high fitness level can "get by" on less than that due to their body's ability to reach the deep-sleep portion of their sleep cycle faster and remain there longer than the rest of us. This results in a longer period of good quality sleep although the entire sleep period is shorter than that of someone sleeping eight hours.

Many of us readily admit we don't get the daily recommended amount or a good night's sleep. This equates to poor *quantity* and *quality* of sleep, both of which are critical to not only health and overall well-being, but also to performance.

On average, how much nightly sleep do you get? _____

Are you okay with that? Why or why not?

_____

_____

_____

_____

_____

_____

_____

_____

_____

What distinction is there between how much sleep you get on weeknights versus the weekend? What accounts for this?

_____

_____

_____

_____

_____

_____

_____

How would you describe your overall *quality* of sleep?

_____

_____

_____

_____

_____

_____

_____

In the chart that follows, for each of the sleep disruptors listed, circle whether it is an issue for you. If it's an issue, circle how you would categorize the issue. Use the blank spaces to add in any other sleep disruptors that aren't listed here.

Sleep Disruptor	Is It an Issue? Y or N		Extent of Issue
work-related pressure	Y	N	slight issue frequent issue chronic issue
health-related circumstances	Y	N	slight issue frequent issue chronic issue
new family addition	Y	N	slight issue frequent issue chronic issue
room/body temperature	Y	N	slight issue frequent issue chronic issue

Sleep Disruptor	Is It an Issue? Y or N		Extent of Issue
television-watching habits	Y	N	slight issue frequent issue chronic issue
nightmares	Y	N	slight issue frequent issue chronic issue
noise pollution	Y	N	slight issue frequent issue chronic issue
snoring partner	Y	N	slight issue frequent issue chronic issue
frequent urination	Y	N	slight issue frequent issue chronic issue

Sleep Disruptor	Is It an Issue? Y or N		Extent of Issue
eating too close to sleep time	Y	N	slight issue frequent issue chronic issue
	Y	N	slight issue frequent issue chronic issue
	Y	N	slight issue frequent issue chronic issue
	Y	N	slight issue frequent issue chronic issue

Upon your review of the completed chart, what are your key take-aways? Record your thoughts.

_____

_____

_____

_____

_____

_____

_____

The following strategies, compiled by busy professional women just like you, are designed to improve quantity and/or quality of sleep. Circle each strategy that you'd classify as do-able for you. (They are not listed in any particular order.)

- Read a boring book (non e-version) before bedtime

- Banish television from the bedroom

- Banish technology from the bedroom (i.e., smartphone, laptop)

- Drink warm milk or decaffeinated herbal tea before bedtime

- Exercise 1-2 hours before bedtime

- Use visualization

- Practice meditation or mindfulness

- Light scented candles

- Use scented sheets and pillowcases

- Place essential oils on your body's pulse points

- Listen to soft and relaxing background music

- Have a glass of wine

- Use programmable ambient lighting that mimics sundown and sunrise

- Use a machine or app that plays nature sounds (i.e., waves, rainfall, etc.)

- Engage in physical intimacy with your partner

- Get a relaxing massage

- Enjoy a bubble bath

What additional strategies can you list? Record them here.

_____

_____

_____

_____

_____

_____

_____

_____

Keeping in mind a connection with your purpose, how will you benefit from adequate sleep quantity and quality?

_____

_____

_____

_____

_____

_____

_____

Outline a general plan of action to optimize your sleep.

_____

_____

_____

_____

_____

_____

_____

Battle Plan #25 Banishing "Sleep-Shaming"

Imagine if, during a team lunch, one of your colleagues casually mentioned that she got eight hours of sleep the night before. Based on your work culture and what you know of yourself and your team members, what reactions do you think she might receive?

Consider some sample responses below that illustrate the ways in which people get sleep shamed at work when they are transparent about being fully rested. Place a check (√) next to each one you've heard said (either by you or others). Please note that each includes a corresponding subtext.

_____ "Must be nice to get that much sleep." — *Envy veiled in sarcasm*

_____ "Sounds like you're slacking off." — *Slacking off at work—which makes someone a "slacker"*

_____ "How did you manage that?" — *Surprise coupled with sincere curiosity about how anyone could be in a senior management role and get that much sleep*

_____ "I can't even remember the last time I got that much sleep." — *A longing for and reminiscence of how good it is to get real sleep*

_____ "Were you sick or did you oversleep or something?" — *Disbelief that getting seven hours of sleep could be intentional, given the demands of the work*

What is the impact of sleep-shaming?

_____

_____

_____

_____

_____

What would be an acceptable response to someone who shares that she got seven or eight hours of sleep?

_____

_____

_____

_____

_____

_____

_____

How can you be a "sleep ally" when you hear sleep-shaming occurring around you? What can you say or do?

_____

_____

_____

_____

_____

_____

_____

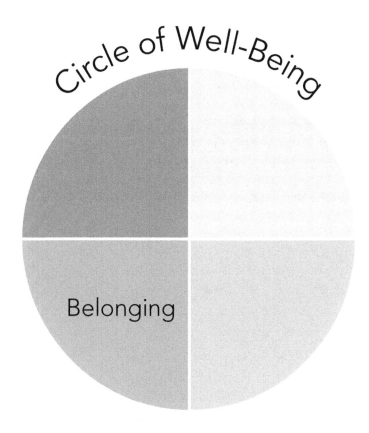

Circle of Well-Being

Belonging

Battle Plan #26 Accruing Your Crew

Thanks to social media, people seem more connected now than ever before. Yet, while there can be an appearance or illusion of connection on the outside, there may be a feeling of isolation on the inside. Outside of social media connections and "friending," who remains? Take a moment and identify your real network of friends. Be sure to include those with whom you may have lost touch.

10 Closest Friends Outside of Work	10 Closest Friends at Work
1.	1.
2.	2.
3.	3.
4.	4.
5.	5.

10 Closest Friends Outside of Work	10 Closest Friends at Work
6.	6.
7.	7.
8.	8.
9.	9.
10.	10.

Describe your reaction to seeing your lists:

_____

_____

_____

_____

_____

_____

What is your definition of a friend? What attributes do you look for in a friend?

_____

_____

_____

What are some ideas for jump-starting a friendship that has lapsed?

_____

_____

_____

_____

Sure, you can do life solo, sans friends, but why would you if you don't have to? If you like the idea of providing mutual support, basking in encouragement, venting your frustrations without judgment, and more, it might feel quite good to have friends in your life with whom you can be real and laugh and cry.

One note about small children: they are truly adept at making friends. It seems to come quite naturally to them. For adults, though, not so much. But if you want to grow your network of friends, you can develop the skill.

Based on your definition of "friend," what can you do to increase your chances of making new friends? Here are a few ideas to get you started.

- Host a monthly book club in your home and ask each invited guest to bring a friend

- Invite someone at work to join you for lunch

- Sign up for and attend a group in your area and attend regularly

What one thing will you do to improve your chances of adding a new friend to your network?

_____

_____

_____

_____

_____

_____

_____

Battle Plan #27 Pre-Loving Your Neighbor

You wave to them whenever you see them at the mailbox or whenever you both are pulling your vehicles into the driveway. They are the neighbors who live next door, across the street, or perhaps two houses over. You've never officially met them and don't even know their names. The odds are, they don't know yours either.

Before you can love your neighbor, it helps to first know your neighbor.

Using their house's location as part of the identifier, list any neighbors you do not know that you would like to know:

_____

_____

_____

Here are a few ideas to help you get to know your neighbors:

- Attend neighborhood events

- Spend more time outside

- Offer to help or loan a tool when your neighbor is involved in an outside task

- Ask to borrow something

- Host a neighborhood barbecue or block party and put flyers on neighbors' doors

What one thing can you do to start building a relationship with your neighbors?

_____

_____

_____

Battle Plan #28 Getting Out of Your Own Way

Does your life—both personally and professionally—include connections and relationships that bring you joy? Or does your life refl ect a one-sidedness that veers toward what I call the three A's—accomplishing, achieving, and acquiring?

Is there anything in your life that you have allowed to get in the way of your relating with others? Sometimes this question is hard to get at because you can be too close to really see. One comedian emphasizes an inconvenient irony with an anecdote about a mother who was reading a variety of books on good parenting in an attempt to improve her parenting skills. In her zeal and enthusiasm, she threw herself into the books with a frenzy every evening after work. One evening, her eight-year-old son pleaded with her to put down her books and play with him. In an exasperated show, she replied, "I can't right now, sweetie. I'm studying how to be a better mom."

Oh, the irony. Think about any of your missed opportunities to connect. Create a list of what you have allowed to get in the way.

"I can't right now. I'm working on…"

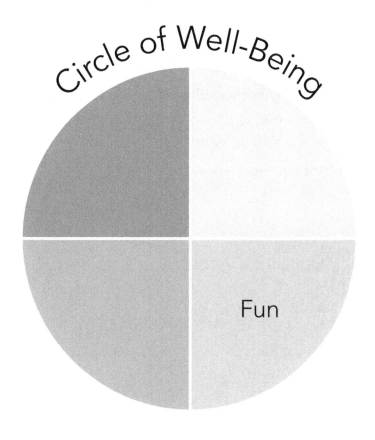

Circle of Well-Being

Fun

Battle Plan #29 Working on Fun

Have you ever watched a group of kids playing on the playground or passed by a school-yard when the kids are outside for recess? If so, you likely heard plenty of happy screams and peals of laughter. It's hard not to smile when children are at play. It makes us feel good to witness it. However, when it comes to adults, fun can be under-rated despite a number of studies that prove otherwise. But studies aren't needed to convince you of the benefits of fun. You only need to consider your own experiences with it.

Recount your most recent fun experience:

When was it? _____

Where was it? _____

What was it? Describe it.

_____

_____

_____

Who else participated?

_____

_____

What made it fun?

_____

_____

_____

How did you feel during it?

_____

_____

_____

_____

For how long after it was over did you feel that way?

_____

_____

_____

What is the benefit of having fun on <u>purpose</u>?

_____

_____

_____

_____

_____

_____

_____

Battle Plan #30 Finding Your Fun Type

In his book, *Play*, Dr. Stuart Brown outlines five of what he calls *play archetypes*. Take a look at the following chart for descriptions and examples of each archetype. Circle what you consider to be your primary fun type and your secondary fun type.

Play Archetype	Description	Examples
Rough-and-Tumble	Active play without set rules and structure	Scavenger hunts, dodge ball, tug of war, diving
Ritual	Board games, activities, and sports with set rules and structure	Chess, checkers, monopoly, twister, basketball, tennis
Imaginary	Activities that foster imagination and creativity	Coloring, painting, scrapbooking, acting, improv classes

Play Archetype	Description	Examples
Body	Activities that get the body out of gravity	Yoga, riding roller coasters, mountain climbing, surfing, snorkeling
Object	Activities involving the manipulation, building, and designing of objects	Jenga, Legos, model airplane, snowball fight

What's your primary fun type? What, if anything, surprises you about your type?

_____

_____

_____

What's your secondary fun type? What, if anything, surprises you about your type?

_____

_____

_____

Create a list of fun activities. Include activities beyond your primary and secondary fun types. For each activity, identify the archetype. Take note of themes and patterns.

Activity: _____   Archetype: _____

Activity: _____   Archetype: _____

Activity: _____   Archetype: _____

Activity: _____   Archetype: _____

Activity: _____   Archetype: _____

Activity: _____   Archetype: _____

Activity: _____   Archetype: _____

Activity: _____   Archetype: _____

Activity: _____   Archetype: _____

Activity: _____   Archetype: _____

Activity: _____   Archetype: _____

Activity: _____   Archetype: _____

Activity: _____   Archetype: _____

Battle Plan #31 Rediscovering Your Inner Kid

Do you remember how much fun you had playing as a kid? Do you remember when you stopped playing? It was probably somewhere between childhood and adulthood when life got more serious, and you took on the responsibilities of adulthood. Adult "free" time often consists of binge-watching a favorite show or playing on a smart-phone, instead of child-like energizing and invigorating fun.

There's no such thing as being too old or too busy or too serious to play and have fun. If playing has been missing from your life, it could be that you feel limited by self-consciousness. But do you really care what others might think or say? Or do you care more about how playing will make you feel? Rediscover your inner kid by engaging in regular quality play that lifts your mood, makes you laugh, and elevates your spirit. You'll discover that the more you play, the better you feel.

When I was a kid, I enjoyed group-play such as hopscotch, jacks, tag, and Simon Says. I also enjoyed activities that I could do alone such as cartwheels, jump roping, and hula-hooping. How about you?

What two group-play activities did you enjoy as a kid that you might still enjoy (with little or no modifications)?

_____

_____

_____

What two solo-play activities did you enjoy as a kid that you might still enjoy (with little or no modifications)?

_____

_____

_____

Battle Plan #32 Laughing Your Ass Off

"One minute of deep belly laughter is the equivalent of a ten-minute cardiovascular run." That's a myth I heard several years ago, and though it is not scientifically proven, it continues to inform how I approach the power of laughter. Deep belly laughter is the laughter that doubles you over and convulses through you. It can even bring you to tears. Once you're spent from that kind of laughter, it feels like you've just had a workout! That's why I believe that you can laugh your ass off. Plus, I don't know about you, but I'd rather be laughing than running!

So how can you laugh more in your life? You can increase your chances of getting more laughter in your life by being intentional about what you find laughably funny.

Based on what you know about your funny bone, add to these ideas for getting more laughter into your life. Circle the ideas that appeal the most to your funny side.

Ways to Add More Laughter	
Watch videos of small children laughing	Watch videos of pets doing funny things
Attend a comedian's stand-up act	Invite a funny colleague to lunch
Attend a karaoke night	Join a laughter club
Play with small children or a puppy	Watch funny shows like "Kids Say the Darndest Things"

Part II: Self-Advocacy

self-advocacy

/self 'ad və kə sē/

the act of speaking up and speaking out on behalf of yourself in order to make known your wants and needs and to advance your interests and views

Battleground

I grew up in a household of four females—my strong and supportive single mother raising her three daughters. My mother taught my two sisters and me to be strong and supportive of each other as well, and she led us to believe that there was nothing we couldn't accomplish. We learned from her that the world outside isn't fair; we'd have to be at least twice as good to be considered half as good as men (black-girl tax not included).

It didn't take long before I learned that my mother was right. Even when I was young, my uncle gave me the nickname "Boss Lady" because I didn't fit the mold of what he thought girls were "supposed" to be. In some circles, being a "boss lady" signifies "aggressive," "opinionated," and "unnatural." Yet, when "boss" qualities are exhibited by men, they are lauded as "assertive," "decisive," and "leader-ly." My love-hate relationship with that moniker continues today.

This is but one example of the different standards and the different rules that exist for men and women.

Just recently, a female account manager at a Fortune 500 company was verbally reprimanded by her male manager for being "too emotional." Apparently, during a one-on-one meeting, she informed him that she had a lot on her plate, but when he observed her later that day helping out a colleague, he considered her assessment exaggerated. As if helping a colleague negates the validity of her assessment of her workload.

Instead of seething and staying silent, she spoke up—to him and to Human Resources. As a result, the matter was addressed in her favor, and rightly so. The lesson here is that speaking up does not make you a troublemaker. *It makes you brave.*

Whether it's speaking your truth or calling out wrongs, your voice is your power.

And every time you lift it, you disrupt the status quo, you spark change, and you pave the way for others. Even if you're the only one at the table saying it, there may be a chance you're not the only "woke" one thinking it. But even if so, you can be the voice of impact for those not represented at the table.

The reality of the world in which we live is that managers, customers, and clients always seem to expect a "Yes." But if you don't recognize it and respond to it in a healthy way, your work will continue to grow more all-consuming as you work harder and harder to get more and more accomplished—at the same time, expecting to be recognized and rewarded according to your contributions and worth.

The previous section on well-being was designed to ground you in finding and developing your inner strength for self-advocacy. When you focus on it and channel it outward with the aim of speaking and acting on your own behalf, you're more than halfway there.

Self-advocacy, like well-being, is a skill that you can practice and gain more mastery of. Many women, though, describe self-advocacy as a "fight" because of how they feel. It feels like a battle to get their voices heard and seriously regarded in certain environments and to take on behaviors that may feel unnatural or uncomfortable in order to compete. Added to this is the reality that these same behaviors are the ones for which women are often condemned and for which men are praised.

So, be proactive. Make waves. Speak up. According to Pulitzer Prize-winning historian Laurel Thatcher Ulrich, "Well-behaved women rarely make history." You make history not when you stay quiet, but when you speak up. Will you decide it's worth it? If it is, blow the time-out whistle and shout out, "Hey! See me! Hear me! That's out of bounds! What gives?"

Because others' reactions to your self-advocacy may be mixed, it's of real benefit to you to first get grounded on what self-advocacy might look like, sound like, and feel like for you.

I asked my ten warriHER co-authors to share their thoughts about and experiences with self-advocacy. As you "listen" to each of them, take note of what resonates with you.

WarriHER Wisdom on Self-Advocacy

WarriHER Wisdom on Self-Advocacy
Baylie

To me, self-advocacy means prioritizing myself and my goals in life. I always say, "If you don't go after what you want in life, someone else will." I like to remind myself of this in order to hold myself accountable in both my personal life and my career. Personally, I've never had a problem vocalizing my goals and expectations to others.

It's hard to pinpoint what strategies work because self-advocacy comes naturally to me. I think it starts with just having a go-getter mentality, a can-do attitude, and the ability to stand up for what I feel most passionate about. Being able to properly vocalize while being cognizant of my audience is the key to self-advocacy.

Earlier this year, I was eligible for a promotion, and I made sure that I shined in front of leadership. In the months leading up to my review, I had a check-in with my boss to get her perspective on my progress and to communicate that I felt ready for a promotion, given my performance. I was very clear in verbalizing my expectations. After surpassing all of my sales targets and having a nearly perfect review, the promotion did not happen. I was not given any substantial reason why.

At that moment, I realized that, while I had been strongly advocating for myself, my boss had not. I expressed my dissatisfaction. Luckily, I was able to successfully self-advocate while interviewing at other companies and ultimately received an offer for a senior level role.

WarriHER Wisdom on Self-Advocacy
Carrie

I (and any person) am most powerful when my thoughts, actions, and emotions are driven by love and truth. Self-advocacy is the result when I truly am acting with love for myself and am true to myself. It's critical to understand this because self-advocacy is a result.

This might sound really aspirational and theoretical, so consider the example of Beth. Beth knows she needs to change some of her eating habits. But she loves food, and her family has a really fun time making a yummy but not-so-healthy dinner every Friday. Beth doesn't want to give this up so she tells herself that she can't change Friday because of her family. They would be so disappointed!

Beth goes through Friday after Friday enjoying the food and time, but deep down feels disappointed in herself. She tells herself that she is doing it for the family and that she doesn't have a choice. However, she's never talked to her family about making a change or offered any alternatives.

In this example, Beth has made herself powerless by not doing the most loving thing for herself and by not being truthful with herself. And she didn't advocate for herself!

I know this example well, because I've lived it. And I could give you similar examples both personal and professional.

Here's how I have been able to change and advocate powerfully for myself.

First, excuse-free honesty with myself. What I really want, believe in, and know in my heart is true. This is tricky, because as I've become more self-aware, I've become sneakier with my excuses. It's so easy to rationalize not making the hard call, taking the most vulnerable path, or speaking out when I know others won't be happy. To get honest, I meditate, journal, and talk to people I trust and know will challenge me to advocate for myself.

Second, when the biological fight-or-flight response kicks in, I don't ignore it or try to resist it. Instead I observe and remind myself of all the facts. What will happen if I don't advocate for myself? My brain and body are excellent at telling me all the bad things that will happen if I take the normal stand-down-don't-rock-the-boat-keep-the-peace course of action. I have to train my brain to see the other risks that are so great: loss of power, diminished self-respect, and self-loathing.

A few years ago, I left my partnership at an international firm to go on a quest to do work with deep meaning that would give me the freedom to live the life I wanted to live. I didn't have a job, business, or title other than "in transition."

Through that journey to take that step and then completely change my life and work, I have identified one issue that is at the root of all challenges.

Worthlessness.

Yes, I was a partner at one of the "Big Four" public accounting firms and on paper had reached an elite level of success. But deep down, I felt worthless in so many ways. And in my work with women and men, I find that deep and hidden feelings of worthlessness are at the root of so many shattered dreams, not-quite-making-it, plateauing, health crises, addictions, and pain.

I was shocked when I recognized my deep feelings of worthlessness. I never expected this challenge! But realization (truth again!) gives me the power to overcome, and I continuously challenge myself to uncover actions, feelings, and beliefs that are rooted in worthlessness—and reframe them.

My first realization of worthlessness came when I told my husband that I had to start my quest. I was the primary earner and was convinced that he would tell me I couldn't leave. And, when I was really honest with myself, I had a deep feeling that maybe he wouldn't love me as much if I didn't have a big paycheck and a title.

He blew my mind when he said, "You've been so successful doing something you're not passionate about, so imagine how successful you'll be when you are doing work you love." In an instant, my life changed. I was free to be myself, and I didn't have to buy love with money or achievement anymore.

WarriHER Wisdom on Self-Advocacy
ChrisTiana

Recently, a disability justice organization reached out to ask if I would sit on a panel alongside some other disability justice advocates for a day-long conference. The pitch for my presence on the panel did not come with a request for speaking rates. When I asked if they had a budget for stipends, the organizer shared that they had never paid people to work the conference and had assumed they would volunteer their time. Im-mediately, I contacted a close friend who sat on their board. They had already shared their frustration over the lack of stipends and how their attempts at making participation equitable seemed to be largely ignored. In that moment, I had a choice.

I could self-advocate for payment. After all, I knew the conference really wanted me to sit on the panel, and I was confident I could negotiate my asking price. On the other hand, I thought about the others who would be sitting on the panel or working the conference with me—unpaid. The choice was clear. I told the conference organizers I would not be able to commit to the conference unless there was payment. Only a couple of weeks later, I was informed that payment was secured for all participants of the conference. I was excited, but needed to know: Was everyone else getting paid as well? Yes! In fact, my friend later called and shared that my advocacy had helped kick-start a conversation about compensation and will likely lead to a change in the future.

With any "self-advocacy," I reflect on the ways in which I am marginalized or oppressed and try to develop strategies on how to find parity in my situation by addressing the larger, systemic, meta issue. As my grandma used to say, "From a tiny spark may burst a mighty flame."

WarriHER Wisdom on Self-Advocacy
Harriet

Self-advocacy means making sure my needs are being supported. That starts with articulating what my needs are—to myself and to my family. I hold myself accountable to this by actually scheduling time to take care of myself. Whether that's getting a massage, going to the mall alone, or meditating. Just as I would schedule time for other priorities such as meetings at work, doctor appointments for my daughter/father/husband, scheduling time on my calendar makes it "more real."

As for my family, it's continuing to reinforce the importance of my needs. Sometimes it's as simple as "it's now about Mom, not about you!"

WarriHER Wisdom on Self-Advocacy
Jemia

Being my own champion is what the word self-advocacy means for me. It's not waiting for someone to mention my name in a meeting or for that tap on the shoulder. It's about taking ownership of my success, career, and development.

I consider myself a self-advocacy strategist because I have become the person people approach to talk about strategies on how to advance in various stages in their lives. I am an out-of-the box thinker, and that has helped me propel my career and personal projects.

I like to connect with the person who is under the radar. I don't mean a person who is not considered a leader or top performer. What I mean is that I look at the person who is well-connected but not the person at the top. When people are trying to build a name for themselves at work, they want to build relationships with the decision-makers first. But what about the people that surround the decision-makers?

I also never stop networking. It sounds obvious, right? Well, not really. Once you achieve status at work or enter the right career circle, you might believe your job is complete. But it is just getting started. Companies evolve and positions change.

Never feel that your current network of people is good enough. Once I start to feel like I have arrived, my next thought is to look for new groups with which to connect.

Never stop advocating for yourself because when others stop advocating for you, which they will, you are all that you have left. And when you are all you have left, it's then you realize that well-being and self-advocacy go hand-in-hand, a lesson I learned the hard way.

There was a time I was over-worked, stressed, and unhappy with more than one thing in my life. I became engulfed in making things happen and stretching myself too thin by over-promising on tasks at work and on personal projects. Then I had to tell my leaders I can no longer be a part of a project I was leading, and I had to say to a publication that I could no longer contribute articles at the level we had discussed. I felt defeated, like a failure, and that I would not be asked again to be a part of projects. It was not a good feeling.

I was too exhausted to even want to think about advocating for myself. I would sit in a room with essential people, and it was almost like I was a shell of a person. My mentors and advocates would work hard to get me a seat at the table only to turn around and have me show up and not be the person they knew I was.

However, when I took a step back to focus on my well-being, the articles I wrote were better than before. For the meetings I led, I was more prepared than ever. The time I took to pull myself out of challenging moments allowed me to reset and rethink my priorities. It allowed me to focus better. I progressed from a "Yes" woman to an "I will get back to you with my decision" woman.

WarriHER Wisdom on Self-Advocacy
Laura

Advocating for ourselves is something many women are directly trained not to do. Even as little girls, we are told to be quiet, listen to everyone else, put our feelings aside, and rely on the opinions of others to form our sense of self. We dress, speak, and act in the way that society decides is most acceptable for us. Self-advocacy requires that we unlearn these narratives and speak up for what we need and deserve.

This is true at work, at home, and in our communities. No one knows what we truly need except us. Whether it's more challenging work, more downtime, or to be seen in ways we are being rendered invisible, we have to be our best and biggest advocates.

On the other side, we cannot ask this of women without offering tools for learning how to self-advocate. We need to teach adult women how to speak up for their needs and set firm boundaries for the first time. And we need to teach young women and girls how to go against the narrative that their needs come last. Only by teaching and modeling these behaviors can we create a future where self-advocacy is seen as normal.

In my own life I have had to learn how to vocally put my dreams, desires, and boundaries in the forefront of all arenas of my life. I got married very young, and I married a man I met in church, who then used our religious beliefs to justify his abusing me. He made sure I did not feel empowered in my finances, my career, my sexuality, or my faith.

Of course, he covered up his controlling behaviors by appearing to be encouraging and supportive at certain times. This kept me continually confused and forced me to put my voice on mute and shift my needs to the side. I spent the emotional energy I could have used to grow myself as a whole person and used it to keep him calm.

Even outside of domestic violence situations, women can feel similarly depleted in this way. I grew up surrounded by women who never put their needs first. They always took care of everyone's needs, i.e., working outside the home, cleaning, cooking, feeding, and budgeting, without ever asking for their turn. They bragged about eating cold food and sleeping only a few hours a night because they thought it made them better wives, mothers, and women. This culture was toxic no matter how well intended it was. Women have to learn that it is not selfish to demand that our energy be invested back into ourselves. In fact, it is the best way to ensure we can be there for others.

WarriHER Wisdom on Self-Advocacy
Mayerland

I have always believed that it's vital to have a credible advocate to grow your career within a corporation. To be clear, an advocate is not typically your mentor, but the person who can best promote your abilities and potential to those who make the decisions on your career.

However, when I was in a difficult place in my career, it was my mentor who told me that it was time to self-advocate. She said, "No one can represent you as well as you can, so why do you keep allowing others to speak for you?"

Up until that point I had strongly believed that it was more powerful to let others toot your horn. It was true… until it wasn't. I got to a place where my advocate was recommending options that worked better for her than for me. The decision-makers believed that those were my wishes. I had to sidestep my boss and meet directly with the decision-makers to make my desires clear. I also had to contradict some of the things my advocate had shared, which was also difficult, as my advocate at that time was my boss. I stayed transparent with my advocate/boss and let her know I was speaking to those above to share my career interests—as I knew she would hear about it anyway.

What worked for me was sharing my aspirations and my disappointments in a non-emotional way to communicate what I was willing to sacrifice to achieve those goals.

WarriHER Wisdom on Self-Advocacy
Nani

I had heard self-advocacy being described as knowing yourself, knowing what you need, and knowing how to get it. That sounds pretty straightforward but not as easy to put into practice. For me, it took time to discover my voice. I have learned that self-advocacy has to start with self-awareness and self-love. I had to recognize my own value and believe that I deserve whatever it is I am fighting for.

The best way for me to self-advocate is to allow time to reflect and be clear about what I want and why. I have to be honest about my intentions and address any fears that may stand in the way. In some cases, it may require me to learn what my rights are and what I am entitled to. Information is critical and allows me to act on facts rather than on emotions alone. Having trusted mentors and friends are also valuable and serve as a sounding board and support. However, I do limit outside advice so that I can stay true to my own convictions and needs.

I have been in compromising situations where I felt mistreated and violated by clients and colleagues. Although I spoke up and addressed it head on, I was too quick to let it slide and forgive. Instead of expressing outrage, I was trying to make light of the awkward situation by being quick to show understanding and letting them off the hook too easily. If I could go back for a re-do, I would make my point more clearly so that they would never mistreat me or any other woman.

I also believe there are some things that are not worth the fight. There have been times when, after assessing the situation, I was okay with letting it go. It wouldn't be worth it if there is a chance it could isolate myself or others and affect relationships or trust. I have to do a full analysis of what I would gain versus what I would lose.

In a team setting, as important as it is to advocate for myself, I have to be cognizant of how my choices affect the team and the organization. This takes self-control, maturity and awareness (self and team). I prefer to look at the situation from all angles before acting.

Growing up as the youngest of seven children in a Korean household provided me with many rich cultural experiences but I have done my share of testing, challenging, and pushing boundaries set by my culture. I was a tenacious and a very determined little girl who wanted to be taken seriously in a house full of older siblings. Having five brothers was like having five father figures hovering over me.

I tried to emulate my only sister who is creative and quiet, and who embodies "true femininity." She showed me how to "behave like a lady." I observed the dynamics between the genders and the birth order. Culturally, we were taught to respect and honor our elders, even if it's just by a few months.

As the baby girl in the family, I knew I had a lot to prove to earn respect. Fortunately, my parents taught us to "live in harmony," to respect everyone, and to be compassionate, kind, and humble. It wasn't hierarchal, but I did sense that the boys had more freedoms and adventures, which I admired.

When we immigrated to the United States, our "harmony" was disrupted as our tight family unit was faced with many unknowns and new obstacles. We had to learn to assimilate to a new culture, learn a new language, and embrace new experiences. Stepping outside for the first time, it was as if we suddenly lost our voices. I felt invisible while feeling like I stood out as well.

We were now considered the "other" and different.

My father who was a scholar, a respected journalist, and an on- air personality in Korea was being treated like a nobody and spoken down to because, when you don't speak fluent English, it's assumed you're not educated. I wanted so badly to speak up for him and for us, but I didn't know how to at the time.

One benefit of being the youngest in an immigrant family is that I was able to learn English quickly and lose the Korean accent. Like many immigrants, we worked hard, not taking anything for granted. My parents modeled for us what it means to be good citizens—supporting various causes and always being willing to give time and resources to help others. It's a beautiful quality.

But I also saw a bit of defeatism when it came to how they were being treated in unfamiliar situations. They didn't want to draw attention to themselves in certain circles or cause any conflict or ignite hate so they just kept quiet. Remember "live in harmony" and peace? This stayed with me throughout my life, especially in my career. I just put my head down, focused on my work, didn't speak up or out, and never rattled any cages.

Once I was in a leadership role, I was expected to speak up for myself, my team, and my clients. I found it easy to advocate for others, but I still felt uncomfortable when it was about me. I was grateful for all the professional development coaching I received on leadership, executive presence, and negotiation skills. Interestingly, these programs showed that I placed a great value on roles and boundaries, not wanting to overstep, and wanting to stay in my own lane.

It took a supportive boss and some colleagues who championed and helped me to gain confidence in my capabilities. They also taught me to set higher goals for myself. I was never timid, but I certainly tempered my aspirations because I didn't think I was allowed to ask for more. Like many women, I felt the need to get permission, as if we don't deserve success. It all sounds silly now.

WarriHER Wisdom on Self-Advocacy
Rhoda

Self-advocacy, to me, is many things.

First, it's knowing myself and my needs, knowing what I want to achieve, and knowing how to achieve it.

It's being able to represent myself. I refuse to allow anyone to speak for me because no one knows best how I feel or want to be treated. No one knows me better than me. For many years, women have been suppressed and told how we should feel. I refuse to live under those conditions.

It's also about being able to present my views and how I perceive things. It's important for me to speak up and contribute to my surroundings, my well-being, and my purpose. Self-advocacy allows me to fulfil that purpose.

It's being true and authentic to what works for me and what doesn't, speaking for and representing myself, and positioning myself to get what I need.

Self-advocacy is about owning my voice and story unashamed.

Two strategies have worked for me. The first is sharing my story regularly. Doing this made me realize my inner power because sharing allowed me to dig deeper personally and resulted in my gaining professional exposure. The second is using my story and the influence that came with it to found Her Story Matters, an organization that builds awareness about social injustice and relies on a collaboration of women's voices.

Being born in Kenya, I faced cultural challenges. In Africa in general, many people don't talk about their issues or challenges. Most things are taboo to speak of and, because of this, people suffer quietly.

In order for me to be who I am today—able and willing to speak about my life with no reserve and expose outdated cultures—I had to overcome a tradition imposed on women that dictates what we say and how we behave. A woman like me would be considered too outspoken and difficult. On top of that, my organization Her Story Matters exposes those limiting beliefs and allows women in particular to be free from that old mindset.

WarriHER Wisdom on Self-Advocacy
Sara

Self-advocacy is speaking up when I feel uncomfortable or need help in a situation, whether it's at work, in a conversation, in a restaurant, in a relationship, or anywhere I happen to be. It can be as simple as asking for some of the lights to be dimmed to accommodate my photophobia—the technical term for my extreme sensitivity to light that causes headaches in normal lighting—or as complicated as going through all the steps to set up formal accommodations through a Human Resources department at work, including doctor appointments, meetings with specialists, and seemingly endless forms.

Self-advocacy is complicated because I don't always know how I feel. This may be true for others and it is part of many people's experience of autism, called interoceptive awareness. As I teach my students, the first step in self-advocacy is to know what you need, and when you don't know how you feel, this can be tricky! So, I have worked to learn how to watch my body for signs of distress and act quickly to make changes in my environment when necessary.

Over time, I can proactively advocate for these things. For someone like me, much of this revolves around sensory issues, such as light, sound, temperature, and proximity to others. So, for example, if I know I will be at a workshop with a likelihood of small group work, I can ask ahead of time for my group to have a break-out room to work in, so that I will be able to contribute without being overwhelmed by the sound of the entire room talking at once. This strategy has worked far better for me than suddenly realizing in the midst of the cacophony that I'm not able to handle it!

Another time that I definitely use self-advocacy on a daily basis is in conversations. Because I use language differently than the typical population does, sometimes I find myself confused by someone else's communication, or, misunderstood in what I'm trying to convey. I have found that letting people know that they should ask me for clarification if they feel offended or confused by something I've said, as I tend to be extremely direct, to the point of blunt at times, which can be interpreted as rude or even hurtful. Conversely, I often will ask for clarification myself when I don't quite understand what someone else is trying to communicate—often because they are implying their meaning rather than being straightforward.

The above strategies work most of the time; however, some people simply don't understand or choose to accept my needs or possibly the needs of others in general. This used to be extremely distressing to me and would often ruin my day. Now in those cases, I am able to take stock more frequently and realize that I have choices to make. Depending on the situation, I can escalate my self-advocacy to a higher authority, perhaps Human Resources, or a manager, for example, or, I can choose self-care, and leave the situation or environment. I have learned over time how to negotiate these situations for my own well-being, and stand up for myself when needed, and move away when that's a better option for me.

Battle Plan #33 Diffusing Saboteurs

"Sticks and stones may break my bones, but words will never hurt me."

This popular childhood refrain that many of us remember all too well is indicative of a paradigm that simply isn't true anymore. In light of what we know about the power of words, our voice and what we convey are a huge part of self-advocacy. Sometimes, though, the words we say to ourselves can sabotage us by derailing our interests and demotivating our spirit. Conversely, the words we say to ourselves can heal, inspire, encourage, and motivate. What we say to ourselves is inextricably bound with what we think, believe, feel, and do and—by implication—what we don't think, don't believe, don't feel, and don't do.

Women especially can inadvertently fall into a habitual pattern of using certain words in ways that are detrimental. Certain words or phrases in particular drive inaction. Let's call them "saboteurs." Take a look at some common saboteurs that follow and see how they can be blockers to self-advocacy.

Circle all the saboteurs you've used over the past six months to a year:

Saboteurs	Description	Usage Examples
"as soon as"	a belief that a positive activity or event cannot occur until some other event has first occurred	"**As soon as** things slow down, then I'll…" "**As soon as** the kids go to bed, then I'll…" "**As soon as** I retire, then I'll…"

Saboteurs	Description	Usage Examples
"always"	a belief that no matter what one does, things will still turn out the same	"Even though I work so hard, I'm **always** behind." "Despite hitting all my targets, someone else will **always** get the promotion." "No matter what I do, it'll **always** be this way."
"never"	a belief that improvement in one's circumstances is an impossibility	"Things will **never** get better." "I'll **never** have work-life balance." "My getting more fit at my age will **never** happen."
"but"	a belief that a need or want is necessarily blocked by a circumstance	"I want to have a better work-life balance, **but** my workload is too heavy." "I want to be more fit, **but** I don't have time to make it to the gym." "I need more sleep, **but** I'm a single parent with two active kids."

Saboteurs	Description	Usage Examples
"unless"	a belief that one cannot take action until a prerequisite action occurs first	"**Unless** I get a new manager, I won't be able to…" "I can't ask for a raise, **unless** other women speak up." "**Unless** I lose weight, I can't pursue…"
"try," "might", or "probably"	a belief that opens the door for uncertainty, procrastination, and failure	"I will **try** to exercise today." "This **might** work." "I can **probably** do this."

Diffusing these saboteurs is easier than you think. For example, the words **"although"** and **"will,"** when used in conjunction with each other, can provide both an acknowledgment of your circumstances, which admittedly can be tough sometimes, and a source of self-empowerment and fierce determination, respectively. Here's the template:

"**Although** [your challenging circumstance], I **will** [positive mindset statement or a statement of courageous action you will take].

Examples:

"**Although** it will require much effort on my part, I **will** take better care of myself!"
"**Although** I am under a lot of pressure right now, I **will** achieve my goal!"

In other instances, it's simply a matter of being intentional about eliminating certain words. For example:

"I can **probably** do this."
"I can do this."

What's your plan for minimizing or safeguarding against the use of saboteurs?

_____

_____

_____

_____

_____

_____

_____

_____

_____

_____

_____

_____

_____

Battle Plan #34 Cultivating Your "No"

Just because you can say "Yes" doesn't mean you should. A well-placed "No" can be one of the most powerful tools of self-advocacy, as well as one of the best allies of your well-being. I'm not sure if it's because I'm in my 50's, but I've mastered the fi ne art of striking a balance between caring about people yet not giving a damn what they think of me. If saying "No" causes people to think less of me, then I get to "lovingly" release them from my thoughts and move on, stress-free. The "not giving a damn" thing can work for you, too.

Saying "No" does not make you a "not nice" person. It makes you a wise person. Amidst life's many pressures and demands, saying "No" with confi dence allows you to establish boundaries and manage expectations. It also conveys and affi rms your values and priorities as non-negotiable.

Here are five ways to say "No":

1.   That won't be convenient for me.
2.   I'm uncomfortable with that.
3.   I have a more pressing priority right now.
4.   Maybe some other time.
5.   I'm looking for something else that aligns more with my interests.

What additional ways can you come up with to say "No" that work with your style and personality?

_____

_____

_____

_____

Responding with a "No" that's infused with your style and personality means you've just successfully advocated for your well-being. And when you've got a ready "No" that you can tailor on the fl y, you won't be caught off-guard and feel compelled to default to "Yes."

Based on the situation, it may also be a good idea to offer what I call a "no with options" response for work-related requests. For example, *"I have a more pressing priority right now"* becomes *"That's not convenient for me right now, but I can help once I complete my current project."*

Create a menu of "no with options" that could work for you and your situation .

1. _____

_____

2. _____

_____

3. _____

_____

4. _____

_____

5. _____

_____

Battle Plan #35 Saying Those 3 Words

Saying "I need help" does not mean you're weak. It means you're strong.

We got that wrong initially. Being a "superwoman" is not about doing it all, all by yourself. A "superwoman" defines her own "all" and then does it—with the enduring help and support of others. No doubt, you've heard the expression, "it takes a village." Well, you don't outgrow the village just because you grow up. You curate a tribe of warriHER supporters that help you and that you help, too.

An inability or unwillingness to admit a need for help fosters and perpetuates a false sense of independence and self-reliance that can isolate you. Before you can receive help or give help, somebody has to utter those three words that can be so difficult for some women to say.

I. Need. Help.

Because women are judged more harshly than men, we tend to place great value on "having it together," and we work hard to maintain that image. It's perception management. The higher our career level, and the higher our wealth, the more high-stakes our perception management becomes. With that kind of burden, consider how hard it is to admit a need for help.

What about you? When was the last time you needed help *and* asked for it? Relate the circumstances surrounding your need for help and your decision to seek it.

Battle Plan #36 Surveying Your Ask

"'Help me?' What? I don't need help. Thank you very much."

Have you ever spoken these words or something similar? Strung together the way they are, such phrases can betray fierce independence, extreme self-reliance, and false pride.

In the zeal for gender equality, the "superwoman" was born. She is a force to be reckoned with because her superpower is that "she can have it all." Yet what emerged from the superwoman phenomenon did a huge disservice to women. How can we acknowledge a need or desire for help when we're supporting the "superwomen" who are out there being praised for doing and having it all? Perhaps you've been touted as a superwoman yourself. If so, you know how misguided this paradigm really is.

Here's how it unravels. First, just because women can have it all doesn't mean we want to or have to. Second, the only definition of "all" that matters is your definition. And third, the only definition of "all' that matters is yours! (The point bears repeating.)

It's time to abandon the superwoman model for a more realistic one that affirms the power of community, collaboration, and cooperation with one another. Needing help and asking for help do not imply any moral failing on your part. No one expects you to do life alone. You don't have to. There need not be a huge shift in your circumstances to be reminded of the importance of that.

Circle how you rate each of these eight statements, where 0 means you strongly disagree and 10 means you strongly agree:

Your Ask Personality Survey

1. I hesitate to ask for help for fear of being perceived as incapable
   0   1   2   3   4   5   6   7   8   9   10

2. I hesitate to ask for help because I don't want to burden anyone
   0   1   2   3   4   5   6   7   8   9   10

3. I hesitate to ask for help because I believe in independence and self-reliance.
    0   1   2   3   4   5   6   7   8   9   10

4. I hesitate to ask for help because I don't see anyone else asking for help.
    0   1   2   3   4   5   6   7   8   9   10

5. I hesitate to ask for help because it may count against me for future advancement or opportunity.
    0   1   2   3   4   5   6   7   8   9   10

6. I hesitate to ask for help because it means surrendering my control to others.
    0   1   2   3   4   5   6   7   8   9   10

7. I hesitate to ask for help due to what I might have to do in return.
    0   1   2   3   4   5   6   7   8   9   10

8. I hesitate to ask for help because I don't know how to ask.
    0   1   2   3   4   5   6   7   8   9   10

Reviewing Your Results

Each of the eight statements in your Ask Personality Survey represents one or more issues listed below. Pay particular attention to issues corresponding to statements you rated a 6 or higher.

1. Poor perception management, low self-esteem, low confidence
2. Self-consciousness, catastrophizing, sensitivity
3. Aversion to interdependence, "lone wolf syndrome"
4. Avoidance of risk-taking, lack of independent thinking
5. Future fatalistic mindset, career insecurity
6. Control issues, inability or unwillingness to delegate
7. Negative over-emphasis on reciprocity
8. Lack of skill-set

Do any of your responses to the eight statements surprise you? Why or why not?

_____

_____

_____

_____

_____

_____

_____

What have you discovered or rediscovered about yourself as a result of this survey?

_____

_____

_____

_____

_____

_____

_____

_____

Battle Plan #37 Growing Your Ask

When you're proactive, you create an environment in which it is easier to both seek help when you need it and to accept help when it's offered to you. Check out these strategies.

- Forge relationships with women in similar positions within and outside of your company

- Join a social group

- Set a personal goal impossible to achieve alone

- Perform random acts of kindness for others

- Start a Grow Your Ask (GYA) group

What are some other ideas?

_____

_____

_____

_____

_____

_____

_____

_____

What is the best thing that could happen if you admitted a desire or need for help and support?

_____

_____

_____

_____

_____

_____

_____

Think of a current task or project with which you currently need help. Think of a person who could help you and draft your ask to that person. Be sure to include language that addresses concerns you might have about perception.

_____

_____

_____

_____

_____

_____

What do you think of your ask?

_____

_____

_____

_____

_____

_____

1. Is your ask clear, straightforward, and specific?

    YES   NO

2. Does your ask avoid the use of self-negating language? (*I hate to ask, but...*)
    YES   NO

3. Does your ask avoid playing on the guilt or obligation of the other person? (A neutral ask with no hint of "emotional blackmail" is ideal)

    YES   NO

4. Does the possibility of receiving help already begin to lessen your stress or worry? (The possibility of help should foster a sense of relief)

    YES   NO

5. Will your ask be in person? (When possible, in person is best.)

    YES   NO

If your responses are all "Yes," you are on the right track to asking for help in a constructive way. If you can't answer "Yes" to the first four questions, please consider reworking your ask. Once you have an ask that works for you and that you're happy with, you can use it as a template for other situations. Record your notes here.

Battle Plan #38 "Firing" Your Boss

People don't quit jobs; they fire their boss!

You do not owe your employer loyalty just because you're drawing a salary. It's your right to feel appreciated, valued, and included. If the leadership in your company is consistently underperforming in this area, you owe it nothing and are not obligated to stay. Even if the company's line is on point, lip service without corresponding action is like a stack of three-dollar bills—worth absolutely nothing. You deserve more, and you're worth it. Align yourself with an organization whose leaders clearly demonstrate that its people are unequivocally its most valuable asset.

Have you arrived at the realization that certain practices and behaviors are culturally entrenched and may not change anytime soon? When you make the decision to leave, you're voting with your feet and "firing" your boss.

Is it time to fire your boss?

Circle either "Yes" or "No" to the following questions:

Do you feel disrespected, unappreciated, under-valued, or unsupported by your boss?	YES	NO
Are you constantly complaining about your boss at home to your partner or others?	YES	NO
Are your feelings toward your boss creating a negative impact on your home life, such as your relationships with your partner, kids, or friends?	YES	NO
Do you use derogatory terms for your boss when you talk about your boss?	YES	NO

Do you have feelings of dread or anxiety prior to the start of your work week?	YES	NO
Does your boss deliver more negative feedback than recognition?	YES	NO
Does your boss regularly disregard boundaries between work and your personal life outside of work?	YES	NO
Have you developed a "what's the point?" attitude and hold back from giving your best at work?	YES	NO
Has the stress of work had any negative impact on your health and well-being?	YES	NO
Do you consider a root canal preferable to one-on-one interactions with your boss?	YES	NO

There is no hard and fast rule to tell you if it is indeed time to fire your boss based on the number of times you circled "Yes." For some, an answer of "Yes" to the very first question is all you need. For others, the question about the impact on home life says it all. For yet others still, an answer of "Yes" to any five answers (which is the equivalent of a failing grade) may be what's needed.

The secret about this exercise is this: you've never needed it. You will know when it's time to fire your boss. Hopefully, this exercise provides the confirmation you seek and an extra dose of courage to do so. There is something very freeing about knowing a major decision has been made. Now you can focus your energy on your exit strategy. So, update your resume and work your network in order to secure your next career opportunity. Cheers!

Battle Plan #39 Taking Back Your Vacation

Until such time that your employer follows the lead of companies like Daimler and Thrive Global, who disable their employees' emails during out-of-office periods such as vacation, extended illness, and so forth, you can advocate for your right to be "off the radar" when it comes to work-related emails. Emails continue to be an area of challenge because they are as accessible on smartphones as they are on computers—perhaps even more so. Additionally, employees are often required to provide their smartphone numbers to employers.

Have you ever put your vacation plans on the back burner in favor of accommodating business activities or the competing vacation preferences of your colleagues? Have you ever violated your own email "rule" when you set an automatic out-of-office email notification? Making an exception once is all it takes for others to disregard your notification and still expect you to check and respond to emails. After all, if you're known to have done it in the past, then you're bound to do it again, right? Of course, the idea behind the out-of-office notification is to manage the expectations of others as it relates to when you will respond. Pretty standard in nature, the notification may read like this:

> *I am currently out of the office returning on Monday, November 11,*
> *with no access to email. I will return your email upon my return.*

Now imagine a message like this:

> *I am currently out of the office returning on Monday, November 11.*
> *And though you and I know there is no such thing as having no*
> *access to email because there is ALWAYS access, I am not going to*
> *check my messages. I know the last time I was out of the office, I*
> *checked email anyway and responded to a few, but this time I really*
> *want to mean it. My family is pressuring me to be fully present with*
> *them during these next few days, and I want the same thing—to*
> *enjoy our time together without work creeping in. And so, I will not*
> *be checking email. Really. I will return your email upon my return.*

Or an unconventional, no-holds-barred one like this:

> *Hey. Psst. You and I both know there is no such thing as "no access to email." There is ALWAYS access. But here's the thing—I am away with my husband and two kids on an amazing family vacation that we've been planning for quite some time. I'm sure you can imagine how priceless it is for us to get away, so we can connect with each other and create some incredible memories. I pledged to my family that I would completely disengage from work and be totally present, so I will not be checking email or voicemail at all. Again, not checking. Really. If, however, your matter is truly urgent, and you need my assistance, here is my husband's mobile number: 281-555-5555. Call him and run your emergency by him first so that I might gain his support and forgiveness for violating my promise due to your emergency. I will be back in the office fully recharged and ready to get back to work on November 13.*

This out-of-office message is an example of one that is transparently upfront. It advocates more explicitly for the vacation that you and your loved ones deserve in a relatable manner that elicits understanding.

That "busy people don't fully disconnect from work" doesn't have to be the case for you. Try your hand at crafting an out-of-office message for your next vacation.

Battle Plan #40 Getting Out Ahead of a Vacation

If you absolutely positively must do work or check in while you're on vacation, do it on your terms. You set the conditions. For example, you might decide to inform your team that you'll be online and checking email only once every other day from 10:00 a.m. to 11:30 a.m. (Don't forget to provide the corresponding time zone.)

It also helps if you invest in managing expectations and establishing boundaries before, during, and post vacation. Here are some ideas:

- Schedule vacations well in advance when feasible. This gives you and others time to plan for and transition into your absence from the office.

- Avoid scheduling vacation during especially high peak times that you know about in advance, such as third quarter update meetings and new product kick-off.

- Ditch the generic one and create a very personalized out-of-office automatic reply message, (see previous Battle Plan) and abide by it.

- Before your vacation, schedule a check-in with your manager to discuss and resolve any issues or concerns surrounding your upcoming absence.

- Negotiate with team members so that in the event clients or customers need to reach you, they can be directed to the appropriate colleague who is covering for you. Be sure to include that information in your out-of-office message.

What are other ideas?

_____

_____

_____

_____

_____

Battle Plan #41 Banishing "Mommy-Guilt"

Mommy-guilt remains a big issue for working mothers, and even for women who are not mothers due to the related "superwoman" paradigm. Both have roots in the same issue—women taking on imposed gender standards from others.

So, what can you do about mommy-guilt?

First, identify the people in your life who really matter and factor in their opinions and no one else's. From there, you can design something that works for your situation without being affected by the external noise of others who presume to know what constitutes a "good mother."

But what's next is critical. Begin to recognize that caring is implicit in any kind of guilt. In other words, it's virtually impossible for you to feel guilty about something you don't care about. So, if you're experiencing feelings of guilt, guess what, you can acknowledge those feelings as evidence that confi rms that you are a caring mother and, therefore, a good mother.

Feelings of guilt cannot exist without feelings of deep caring. The greater the guilt, the greater the capacity for caring. Please let that sink in and celebrate that. You may even have to say it out loud to yourself multiple times to counteract the garbage we internalize from the outside. Something like: "I feel guilty because I care deeply—and caring deeply makes me a good mother. As a good mother, I reject the guilt."

I'm no psychologist, but it seems as if not enough attention has been paid to this aspect of the psychology of guilt, especially when it comes to ridding mommy-guilt from the lexicon altogether!

Guilty feelings cause unwarranted shame and trap working mothers in a cycle of inaction that exacerbates the shame. It's a brutal cycle. Take heart, though, because you can interrupt the cycle.

How?

Here's an example from my own experience.

When both my kids were heavily into sports, I experienced mommy-guilt because I couldn't attend every single game due to my work. I felt like I was a horrible mother because I wasn't fully supporting them by being there and cheering them on.

I finally grew tired and angry enough at feeling that way that I decided to fix it. Focusing on what I could actually control in my life, along with who in my life really mattered, I involved my kids in the fix. We sat down during one of our family meetings with their game schedule of dates. (Yes, family meetings are another great way to connect on issues and make family decisions together.) I asked them to identify which games were the most important for me to attend. To my surprise, they selected a lot less than what I expected! They had never desired or expected that I attend each and every game. It was my own self-imposed pressure, reinforced by societal pressure, that was responsible for my guilt.

My kids had never once viewed me as a bad mother.

Using this model to define what worked for my family was a win-win. My kids felt included and valued in being asked; I felt freed from the external pressure of the definition of a "good" mother as one who attends all of her children's events. To this day, my family's way of communicating with each other insulates us from the judging eyes of others who dare to push their "definitive" narrative on what motherhood should look like, sound like, and feel like.

When you are constantly communicating with loved ones, you get to create something together that is realistic and customized—something that works!

Have you ever experienced feelings of mommy-guilt?

    YES   NO

Have you ever been mommy-shamed? (Experienced the effects of an attempt to make you doubt or question whether or not you're a "good" mother)

    YES   NO

Have you ever been mommy-shamed by another mother?

    YES   NO

Unfortunately, the existence of the third question is a commentary on the extent to which we women have participated in our own oppression. The incessant messages we absorb regarding gender standards, roles, and expectations are all too often internalized.

How can you do your part to end mommy-shaming?

_____

_____

_____

_____

I asked a group of working mothers what types of mommy-guilt they've experienced, and below are some of their responses. Circle those that have ever caused you to feel mommy-guilt. Use the extra spaces to include any experiences you've had that aren't covered here.

- Being the last parent to pick up kids from daycare or an after-school program

- Buying instead of baking something for the school's Bake-a-Thon

- Not attending a school event or sporting event

- Not volunteering to be a "Classroom Mom"

- Not signing up to serve as a chaperone on a school field trip

- Forgetting about or being late to a parent-teacher conference

- Not attending or not joining the PTA

- Sending your kid to school with a Lunchables™ when a lunch from home is required

- Not getting the required supplies your kid needed by the needed-by date

_____

_____

For any instance of mommy-guilt, how could you have turned things around such that mommy-guilt never even had a chance to manifest?

_____

_____

_____

_____

_____

_____

Now, let's consider the first type of mommy-guilt on the list: being the last parent to pick up your kid from daycare or an after-school program. If your child is not yet old enough to realize being the last to be picked up, then recognize that your feelings of guilt stem from what the daycare staff *must* be thinking about you. So, your plan would have to address that.

For example, if possible, plan in advance the days you will pick up your child close to the pick-up deadline and give the daycare staff a heads-up by letting them know in the morning at drop-off or by making a courtesy phone call at some point during the workday. The purpose of the advance notice is to convey thoughtfulness, organization, and consideration—as opposed to a potential perspective of you as a crisis-driven, last-minute emergency type personality. They will understand that "late" pick-up days are strategically planned by you in advance, and they will probably appreciate knowing when to expect it.

If your child is old enough to realize being the last one to be picked up from daycare or an after-school program, enlist the support of the daycare or school staff in making the last half-hour or so of your child's day special with perhaps a privilege, toy, or treat that you arranged way in advance for just such instances. Your stand-by plan can be activated with a heads-up to the staff when you realize that you are likely going to be picking up your child close to the pick-up deadline. The designated privilege, toy, or treat should only be used when your child will be picked up near the pick-up deadline, or it loses its power as "special." The idea is that, while your child may never like or get used to the "late" pick-ups, your child will associate each instance with a corresponding enjoyable privilege/toy/treat.

Think of one instance of mommy-guilt and map out a proactive strategy to short-circuit mommy-guilt before it can take root.

_____

_____

_____

_____

_____

_____

_____

_____

_____

_____

_____

_____

Battle Plan #42 Facing Your Struggles

The deeper issues of our lives always require introspection. Neglecting ourselves keeps us in a state that is contrary to introspection. The contemplation of purpose and meaning, values, work-life fit, physical wellness, happiness, and fulfillment—these are all worthwhile pursuits. Within these moments of communion with our spirit, the mind clutter clears, and we see that we never intended to minimize our well-being or to mute our power by stifling our voice.

Who in your life is holding you accountable for being true to who and what matters? Because your capacity for self-deception and denial greatly increases in proportion to the duration and extent of the pressures and challenges you face, it might prove helpful to surround yourself with truth-tellers and truth-extractors—those "girlfriends" who will speak truth to you, lovingly force the truth from you, and challenge you to live up to your best intentions and deepest values. What values do you want to honor? What people in your life do you cherish? What kind of wife, partner, daughter, sister, aunt, friend, and/or neighbor do you want to be?

No doubt, you have heard the expression, "the struggle is real." It's not a trite truism. There is not one person I've encountered in my life who hasn't struggled with something. Indeed, the struggle is real for each one of us. When it comes to well-being and self-advocacy, I asked my ten warriHER co-authors to share what they continue to struggle with in the areas of well-being and self-advocacy. Here is what each one had to say:

WarriHER Wisdom on the Realness of the Struggle

 **WarriHER Wisdom on the Realness of the Struggle
Baylie**

I struggle committing to too many things and being overwhelmed to where I can't perform to my best potential. Doing this affects me both physically and mentally—physically because I'm staying up late or waking up early to get something done, and mentally because I am stressing and not able to allocate enough "me time" throughout the week to help me decompress.

In addition to overcommitting, I also struggle with knowing when to dial down the self-advocacy. I am such a vocal individual and am typically very comfortable making it apparent how I feel. Because I work in corporate America, I have to constantly remind myself to read every situation before offering my solicited or unsolicited feedback—determining how much and how little information I should share at that moment in time.

# WarriHER Wisdom on the Realness of the Struggle
Carrie

Though I've come so far in many things—feeling worthy and deserving of joy, investing time in habits that make me feel awesome, standing in my power of love and truth, doing work with deep meaning and getting paid great money for it, and not having to work mega hours to "deserve" it—old habits, beliefs, and experiences are hard to break.

For so many years I was in environments where working tons of hours was celebrated and rewarded. Working harder was the cure for anything that wasn't going well. And I allowed myself to get sucked in. I believed and lived by mottos like "life is hard" and "you can't have it all."

People who didn't work as hard as I worked were selfish slackers, and I resented them. Deep down I wondered how it would feel to think it's okay to invest time in things that are important to me and not the firm or how it would feel to think it's okay to invest in the people in my life whom I care about. (Worthlessness again!)

Now, when things aren't going well in my business, I sometimes slip into what I call "grind mode" when I work like crazy to cure the problem. But instead of curing, I get tired, lose my creativity, and focus on my to-do list more than the value I bring. It's not a cure at all; it actually turns bad into worse! Thankfully I recognize this and am getting better and better at dodging grind mode and staying in harmony.

WarriHER Wisdom on the Realness of the Struggle
ChrisTiana

Last week, I had a long conversation with someone who has shown interest in becoming friends. They would be an amazing friend: Sweet, lots in common, and we both are advocates for social equity and justice. But I was scared—scarred perhaps is more like it. I had recently been burned by someone in whom I had placed a large amount of trust, and they broke it along with my heart.

But this person was not deterred by my hesitance and, after sharing stories of how they had been hurt, they asked me what I thought the solution was to the "com-petty-tiveness."

After a few seconds, I began, "You know the Crab Pot theory? The one where the crabs pull down the other crabs?"

They nodded and added, "The pot is not a natural environment for crabs. That is why they are acting out of survival."

I argued back, "But what about fire ants? Have you ever seen fire ants in a flood? They will form layers and layers of interconnected layers around their queens and injured ants, and the ball will roll so ants can take turns being submerged or getting oxygen!"

We both laughed and then sat for a moment in mindful reflection. What about fire ants? What makes fire ants in a flood different than crabs in a pot? Why, when faced with scarcity and adversity, do we pull each other down into the boiling water instead of finding a way to survive collectively together? What will it take to move our society from a crab model to a fire ant movement?

I am still searching for what neutralizes the bile of othering, isolation, and trauma. How can I, as a social creature, exist in a society that is increasingly antisocial? What does it mean to have internal peace and lovingkindness? Where can I find my ball of fire ants to gather around me during such troubling times as these? Hopefully, there are not simply answers that will come with time. Hopefully, there are answers at all.

WarriHER Wisdom on the Realness of the Struggle
Harriet

Guilt! I was born with guilt. It's the Greek Orthodox way for girls growing up. So, I stop and think to myself, "Why am I feeling guilty? Aren't I a good person? Haven't I taken good care of my parents?" Yes, yes, yes!! That reminds me not to feel guilty.

WarriHER Wisdom on the Realness of the Struggle
Jemia

I no longer struggle with well-being as much, but self-advocacy is an ongoing process for me. I've reached a point within my career to where women are seeking me out for advice, help, and support. I am advising women on how to make career moves and connections—something I often thought I wouldn't do at this stage in my career.

My time is being spent differently now. The time I would spend growing my connections is now used to help other women build their relationships. I have to remind myself that my work is not complete. I still need to keep going to get to where I want to be. It's a work in progress, but I would not trade where I am right now for anything.

WarriHER Wisdom on the Realness of the Struggle
Laura

Making time to just enjoy something, without a clear goal, remains a constant struggle for me. I am very much a "Type A," but I also often buy into the capitalistic belief that my worth is measured by my productivity. The more I output, the more I deserve to be loved or even to exist. This is deeply unhealthy and something I very much disagree with on principle. But old habits die hard, so it is something I regularly have to confront within myself.

WarriHER Wisdom on the Realness of the Struggle
Mayerland

My challenge with self-advocacy comes from my strong faith in Jesus Christ. I know that I am to allow Him to fight my battles, but my worldly wisdom tells me that the squeaky wheel gets the oil. At times I wonder if my self-advocacy results in me "trying to" side-step the Lord (now I know I could never actually sidestep Him!) as I did my boss.

Philippians 4:6 says, "Don't worry about anything; instead pray about everything. Tell God what you need and thank Him for all He has done."

It's interesting that the phrase, "God helps those who help themselves" cannot be found anywhere in the Bible… Ah, there's my answer!

WarriHER Wisdom on the Realness of the Struggle
Nani

An internal voice that questions my ambition sneaks up on me at times. I question whether my intentions are to advocate for myself or if I'm just being selfish or greedy. I have to remind myself that it's okay to want the best for myself. I deserve success, joy, fulfillment, and happiness. That's not being selfish; it's just living a full life.

As I am a mother, my focus has and will always be about their well-being. However, the ability to model how I advocate for myself is greater than any advice I can give them. I put their needs before mine most of the time, but it brings me joy and peace to know that they are happy. If it ever feels off, whether they are having a bad day, are exhibiting a bad attitude or acting downright rude, it can drain my energy, but it's an opportunity to grow together through honest conversations.

My biggest struggle is learning to speak up when dealing with aggressive or negative personalities. When there is strong pushback, maybe even threatening in some way, I can either shut down or get emotional. I may doubt myself and my abilities, which can spiral if I am not mindful. I have learned that I don't always have to react immediately. If I have to pause, process, and then speak, that's even more powerful. I am still learning to stand up for myself with strong personalities, but I am grateful I've come this far.

According to Eckhart Tolle in *The New Earth*, "If the thought of lack (money, love, recognition) has become part of who you think you are, you will always experience lack.... You are withholding it because deep down, you think you are small and that you have nothing to give."

WarriHER Wisdom on the Realness of the Struggle
Rhoda

Regarding well-being, I must confess it's achieving work-life balance! I know it sounds strange. But because I love what I do, I am constantly working! I get ideas and concepts watching shows, speaking to people, and even whilst resting!

My work is my destiny! I went through a difficult time with work in which there were so many decisions to be made, and at the time, I was depleted. I had worked hard and pushed the whole year without taking a vacation. By December, I was depleted and didn't want to continue with anything, I had come to a point of feeling helpless because I was exhausted and couldn't strategize for the following year.

Needless to say, it took six months to recover and since then, I make sure I take time out every month for some days just to refuel. If I don't do so, my natural tendency which is work, would take over!

The struggle with self-advocacy will be culture and tradition. It's not a struggle but a challenge imposed on me and my work. For example, there was a time when I was invited to be a guest on a women's show, and we were discussing labiaplasty, and in the process we somehow started talking about female genital mutilation (FGM), about which I am very passionate. I am against it and create awareness of this outdated practice.

As we were speaking about it, the rest of the panelists were quite reserved about how they felt about it, but I wasn't. During the show, we had call-ins, and all of them were men hurling abuse at me and even calling me "yellow" despite my name displayed on the screen. The insults continued until callers finally concluded that I was not African because I chose to speak up against social injustice. So, my challenge is always going to be not fitting in with classic narratives of the African woman.

WarriHER Wisdom on the Realness of the Struggle
Sara

Although I've made tremendous strides in feeling integrated and accepting myself, including my strengths and barriers, I continue to struggle with internalized ableism— the feeling that I should be able to do things that "everyone else" can do, and in the same way that they can do them. I can sink fairly low fairly quickly when someone else's unaccepting opinion of me happens to concur with my own inner feeling of "I should be able to do this," or perhaps worse: "I shouldn't have done that."

And although this is an area that I continually work on with my students, it is still a difficult thing to move beyond myself. When I find myself in this situation, I do my best to tell myself the same things I would tell my students—to look back at what I really believe about myself, at what is really true about me. To learn from any mistakes that I've made, make reparations if needed, and understand that it's perfectly okay to be human, and that it's perfectly okay to be autistic.

To learn to take the time for self-reflection, rather than simply react, is a life-long journey for me, and one that has been extremely rewarding. It doesn't happen without work, though, and I often need to catch myself before I spiral into an unhelpful thought pattern.

WarriHERs and I recognize that it's not easy. It's often a fight to live true to yourself and make your own rules. That's why you are a warriHER. That's why you're holding a playbook filled with Battle Plans. And because it's not easy, it's important to recognize that when you design your own rules, the design should never be about perfection, but about progress.

Answer the following three questions with brutal honesty—as if you were responding to your trusted truth-teller/truth-extractor.

With what in your life are you still struggling?

_____

_____

_____

_____

_____

_____

_____

_____

_____

_____

_____

_____

_____

_____

What in your life within your control do you want to change?

_____

_____

_____

_____

_____

_____

_____

What in your life threatens or competes with your fulfillment?

_____

_____

_____

_____

_____

_____

_____

Battle Plan #43 Owning Up to Your Stuff

I'm a recovering overachiever and a recovering procrastinator. I share that with you for three reasons:

1. This journey called life is not about perfection but progress.
2. It's important to own up to your own stuff. You can't change what you don't acknowledge.
3. I want to convey that these pages are your safe space to be real and get messy about the stuff that impacts you.

Here's a guiding question: What can *I* do for *me* to help and support *me* having the life *I* want?

Before you can take action, you have to understand yourself and why you think and act the way you do. And yes, there will sometimes be external influences such as environment, your upbringing, your conditioning, societal gender rules, norms, expectations, and so forth. But, yet, and still, the question remains: What can you do for you in spite of and in the midst of?

My explanation of—and your self-assessment of—four different profiles can provide insight to help you answer that important question.

Four Profiles

- Overachiever

- Over-Committer

- Over-Accommodator

- Over-Isolator

Overachiever

On a scale of 0 to 10, with 0 being *nothing like me* and 10 being *most like me*, circle the number reflecting the extent to which you are an overachiever. Refer to the traits below to help with your rating.

0   1   2   3   4   5   6   7   8   9   10

Now, circle the specific overachiever traits that describe you:

- Fast-paced and highly competitive

- Perfection is the standard

- Not satisfied with an A if an A+ is possible

- Addicted to adrenaline

- Powers through sickness without slowing down

- Likely to battle chronic health issues such as shingles and nervous breakdowns

- Powers through sickness of family members without slowing down

- Prioritizes performance over health

- Likely to be struck down by burnout

- Motto: *"I will either do it exceptionally well or die trying."*

Record your insights:

_____

_____

_____

_____

Over-Committer

On a scale of 0 to 10, with 0 being *nothing like me* and 10 being *most like me*, circle the number reflecting the extent to which you are an over-committer. Refer to the traits below to help with your rating.

0   1   2   3   4   5   6   7   8   9   10

Now, circle the specific over-committer traits that describe you:

- Over-the-top team player

- Compelled to prove and re-prove self

- Calendar is always full

- Stretches self too thin

- Takes on more even when lacking capacity

- Volunteers for tasks nobody even thought of

- Suffers in silence with resentment

- Prioritizes others' perception over self-worth

- Likely to suffer from FOMO (fear of missing out)

- Will one-up your busy-ness with tales of her own busy-ness

- Motto: *"The more I do, the more important I am."*

Record your insights:

_____

_____

_____

_____

Over-Accommodator

On a scale of 0 to 10, with 0 being *nothing like me* and 10 being *most like me*, circle the number reflecting the extent to which you are an over-accommodator. Refer to the traits below to help with your rating.

0   1   2   3   4   5   6   7   8   9   10

Now, circle the specific over-accommodator traits that describe you:

- Pleaser at minimum; pushover at the extreme

- Inability or unwillingness to say "No"

- Operates with few or no boundaries

- Lacks discernment about when to say "Yes" and when to say "No"

- Wants to be liked

- Over-apologizes often, even when not at fault

- Rarely disagrees in order to avoid conflict or confrontation

- Prioritizes being liked over being respected

- Motto: *"What can I do to make you like me?"*

Record your insights:

_____

_____

_____

_____

_____

Over-Isolator

On a scale of 0 to 10, with 0 being *nothing like me* and 10 being *most like me*, circle the number reflecting the extent to which you are an over-isolator. Refer to the traits be-low to help with your rating.

0   1   2   3   4   5   6   7   8   9   10

Now, circle the specific over-isolator traits that describe you:

- Fiercely independent at all costs

- Needs to keep up appearances

- Obsessively engages in image and perception management

- Inability or unwillingness to ask for help

- Has strong urge to appear strong at all times

- Struggles with delegating

- Likely has bought into the superwoman complex

- Rarely lets guard down

- Has control issues

- Being respected is more important than being liked

- Feels threatened by highly successful women

- Motto: *"I can't risk you detecting any weakness."*

Record your insights:

_____

_____

_____

Once you've rated yourself in each of these four areas, use the four lines below and rank the four styles in priority order starting with the style that is most like you and ending with the one that is least like you. If there's a tie, use your subjective judgment to think about your experiences to break the tie and then proceed to continue to rank them accordingly.

1. _____

2. _____

3. _____

4. _____

What have you discovered or rediscovered about yourself?

_____

_____

_____

_____

_____

_____

_____

_____

_____

10 Strategies for Overachievers

1. Decide what is good enough and what needs to be more than good enough.
2. Practice delegating in small steps and progress slowly from there.
3. Institute a daily pause that gives you space to just be.
4. Woo you! Embark on a love affair with yourself.
5. Stay true to who you are with small reminders of what and who bring you joy.
6. Give yourself periodic breaks during the day to do something just for you.
7. Start using nondual thinking. You're not a success or a failure. While you'll succeed in some areas, and fail in others, sometimes you'll fall in between. Be okay with that.
8. Take a personal day and do no work.
9. Engage in an activity or hobby for which you have little to no skills.
10. Schedule rest on your calendar and keep the appointment.

Why do you push yourself to achieve?

_____

_____

_____

_____

What message do you send your loved ones when you overachieve at work?

_____

_____

_____

10 Strategies for Over-Committers

1. Practice different ways to say "No" without apology.
2. Delegate.
3. Focus on only what you can control and devise strategies from there.
4. Establish clear boundaries and limits, write them down, and review them regularly.
5. When you sense you are about to overcommit, say "Stop" to yourself.
6. Schedule time with yourself and keep it!
7. Put a limit on daily commitments, track it, and hold yourself accountable.
8. Rework a commitment you don't want with one you do.
9. Team up with a support and accountability buddy with similar challenges.
10. Play hooky from work for a day and do anything you want.

Where have you not established boundaries where you need to?

_____

_____

_____

_____

How have you put yourself last when you should have put yourself first?

_____

_____

_____

_____

10 Strategies for Over-Accommodators

1. Stop apologizing so much.
2. Get very real about the distinction between compromise and surrender.
3. Is there a positive WIIFM (What's in it for me?) element? If not, rework it or abandon it.
4. Treat yourself like you treat your best client/customer.
5. Express your needs confidently.
6. Choose more discriminately between minimums and maximums.
7. Implement a balanced give-and-take philosophy.
8. Start journaling your needs and wants.
9. Set priorities and limits.
10. Create an affirmation that you say to yourself when you feel susceptible.

In what areas are you going above and beyond to make things more convenient for others?

_____

_____

_____

_____

What are the costs to your well-being when you consistently place others' needs and wants ahead of your own?

_____

_____

_____

_____

10 Strategies for Over-Isolators

1. Forge friendships with women in similar positions.
2. Join a social group or online chat group.
3. Ask for and accept help from family and friends.
4. Plan a girls' night out or a girls' vacation.
5. Put the same energy into building your personal network of support as you do your professional network.
6. Be with the people you're with.
7. Practice HALT: don't get too hungry, angry, lonely, or tired.
8. Set a personal goal impossible to achieve alone.
9. Volunteer at a homeless shelter.
10. Perform a random act of kindness for a neighbor at work or at home.

In which kinds of situations are you most prone to feeling isolated and alone?

_____

_____

_____

_____

In which kinds of situations are you most prone to letting down your guard and being vulnerable?

_____

_____

_____

Battle Plan #44 Making Over Mondays

Have you ever wondered why Monday is the most hated day of the week? In addition to being the fi rst day that most people head back to work, the day represents getting sucked back into patterns and habits of work that trigger frustration, powerlessness, or resentment. The more you lack a sense of balanced living, the more you'll tend to loathe Monday and all it represents.

Think back to a recent Monday morning that you dreaded prior to its arrival and then dreaded even more when it arrived. Consider all sources for the dread and list them in the chart that follows. For example, a Monday morning meeting that you used the weekend to prepare for might be stressing you. Or maybe it's enduring the long, soul-sucking Monday commute. Or maybe it's the anticipation of that look in your preschooler's eyes during drop-off at school. Or maybe you flat out hate your job or your psycho boss. Don't worry about whether you have control over the source, just list as many as you can remember. The more specific, the better.

Once your list is complete, place a (√) in the ALL, SOME, or NONE column to represent the degree to which you have control over that particular source of dread.

ALL—you have full control over

SOME—you have some control over

NONE—you have no control over

For each ALL source, come up with a way to eliminate the dread.

For each SOME source, come up with a way to minimize the dread. (Monday meetings are mandatory, for example, but the time of day or in-person vs. conference call are some flexible options.)

For each NONE option, come up with a way to minimize the dread. (Your commute may be fixed, but listening to music or a podcast may lift your spirits.)

Choose an upcoming Monday when you'd like to put at least one of your ideas into place. On your mark. Get set... Happy Monday!

Source of Dread	ALL	SOME	NONE	Action You Can Take

Battle Plan #45 Letting Go for Gain

Does your perspective sometimes get so one-sided that you immediately default to thinking that you must "do" something in order to "gain" something? Suppose, instead, that you can "let go" something in order to "gain" something.

Think about the commitments you currently have. These don't include the mandatory commitments related to you or your family's basic needs of food, shelter, or clothing.

List three commitments you'd like to ditch. Create your list with no guilt or self-condemnation.

1. _____

2. _____

3. _____

Now choose one and draft a practical plan to make your ditch-dream a reality. What support do you need? What arrangements do you need to make? What are primary and secondary considerations? How much lead time is necessary? Let the thought of what you'll gain by letting go motivate you during the process.

_____

_____

_____

_____

_____

Battle Plan #46 Igniting Your Badass-ery

Igniting your badass-ery involves exhibiting these courageous behaviors and an unwavering commitment to never stop fighting.

- Showing up as your authentic self in spite of the haters

- Owning your truth, even when it is unpopular

- Speaking truth to power even at great risk

- Controlling your own narrative

- Fighting for what's right and not settling for what's easier

- Calling out systemic bias and inequity

There is yet to be the widespread outrage at the bias and inequities that continue to plague our world that will finally lead to sustainable change. But still, we fight. We fight on the smaller battlefields of our communities, our workplaces, our neighborhoods—and even our homes.

What follows is a series of training scenarios that are based on actual events. Accompanying each scenario is the response with parenthetical commentary. In the space provided, craft how you would address it. The goal is to be prepared in advance so that you will be ready.

Near the end of a meeting, John, the meeting leader, turns to the only woman attendee, and asks, "Beth, can you give us the female perspective?"

Beth responds with, "I notice that you haven't referred to any of the men's comments as 'the male perspective,' John. Why is that?" (This response calls attention to the appropriation of male as "the norm" and misappropriation of female as "outside the norm.")

What would you say or do?

_____

_____

_____

_____

_____

_____

_____

_____

_____

_____

_____

_____

_____

In a meeting of mostly men and only a few women, Karen says, "If we focus on the qualitative data first, it may have more of an impact on our audience." After a few moments, Eric says, "If we share the quantitative first, it won't have the same effect."

Karen responds, "Thank you, Eric, for being an enthusiastic vocal advocate of my idea." (When your idea has been co-opted, the "kill 'em with kindness" approach is especially effective when delivered with a hint of sarcasm.)

What would you say or do?

_____

_____

_____

_____

_____

_____

_____

_____

_____

_____

_____

During a team meeting, while Angie is talking, Mike jumps in for a second time and interrupts her.

In a confident voice, Angie says, "Mike, I'm talking." (The response is short and effective in its use of the offender's name coupled with the omission of words and phrases like "please," "allow me," "I'm sorry, but…," and "excuse me.")

What would you say or do?

_____

_____

_____

_____

_____

_____

_____

_____

_____

_____

_____

_____

_____

Elizabeth, an electrical engineer who designs and fixes missile test sets, was on call when a test set broke. As she was troubleshooting the broken test set, she heard someone behind her say, "See that. If you break the test set, that cute little engineer comes running." It was Bill, the technician supervisor, who was providing new employee orientation to a new male technician.

Elizabeth turns to look at Bill with a pencil poised on her notepad and asks loud enough for the new technician to also hear, "Bill, what is your employee ID number please?" (This response is a combination of funny and "Don't mess with me," so that everyone could "pretend" the inappropriate comment was just a joke, while leaving Bill with real concern that Elizabeth might contact HR.)

What would you say or do?

_____

_____

_____

_____

_____

_____

_____

_____

_____

_____

Xiaolei, newly hired, attended a global team meeting where leaders from several regions had come together. During the introductions, when it was her turn, she gave her name to the group, only to have one of the participants interject with, "That's going to be too hard for us to say. We'll call you Shelly."

Xiaolei firmly repeats, "It's Xiaolei." (This response carries with it the implicit directive that she will not answer to Shelly and will answer only to her name. At the same time, she reaffirms and revalidates her identity.)

What would you say or do?

_____

_____

_____

_____

_____

_____

_____

_____

_____

_____

On an airport shuttle, a stranger directed only one word at Terri: "Smile."

Terri asks, "How many nonsmiling men have you said that to today?" (This response turns it around to highlight the fact that the "smile and look pretty" directive is reserved for women only.)

What would you say or do?

_____

_____

_____

_____

_____

_____

_____

_____

_____

_____

_____

_____

Kristina's friend Robin revealed to her, "My boyfriend made a comment on Facebook about the Women's March in Washington, D.C. He said in his post that all the women who marched were freaks and psychopaths."

Kristina asks, "Why are you still dating him?" (Kristina's response challenges Robin to examine her reason for not separating from someone who clearly subscribes to misogyny.)

What would you say or do?

_____

_____

_____

_____

_____

_____

_____

_____

_____

_____

_____

_____

Maya's male, platonic friend Gary is pretty high up in his company. He made a comment that really bothered her. He said that it's really hard for him to hire a woman that he's attracted to. He told her that, even if she is the best person for the job, he wouldn't hire her because of that. For him, there is a real hesitation due to the attraction.

Maya exclaims, "So you have no control over your d*ck? No control over your thoughts?!" (Maya's response relies on a shocker to match the shocker effect of Gary's revelation that as the decision-maker, he can deny a qualified woman a job at his company based on stupid sh*t.)

What would you say or do?

_____

_____

_____

_____

_____

_____

_____

_____

_____

_____

Liz met with her mentor to talk about the possibility of an upcoming promotion. During the meeting, her mentor informed her that he did not see it as the right time to put her up for the promotion. According to him, it was too early. Liz asked him if she was still viewed as an "A Player." He agreed that she was still an "A Player" and that nothing had changed.

In response, Liz diagrammed the entire previously promoted three classes. She mapped each person and their time to promotion. At the time of promotion, she mapped out the size and scope of the engagement each one was leading. She walked her mentor through it and then overlaid her situation on top of that data. Liz got promoted. (Liz's systematic, data-driven, well-laid-out process for being recognized and promoted demonstrates the importance of knowing and understanding the system better than anyone else, so as to use that knowledge to level the playing field.)

What would you say or do?

_____

_____

_____

_____

_____

_____

_____

_____

_____

Battle Plan #47 The Healing Ouch

"Ouch."

Unlike some four-letter words, this one can heal instead of harm because it creates a space for open communication to occur. The use of "Ouch" encourages dialogue in uncomfortable situations and tends to reduce the occurrence of knee-jerk defensive reactions to accusations such as, "That's sexist," "That's insensitive," or "That's offensive.'

For example, if you are hurt, offended, or otherwise negatively impacted by a comment or action, you could say "Ouch" in that moment. Because "Ouch" is recognized as a term expressing discomfort, pain, and injury, the offender, as well as those in your proximity, will naturally turn their attention to you in order to see what's the matter. With this platform in place, you can indicate your reason for the ouch.

"Your plan penalizes women for taking time off to give birth."
"The decision was made with everyone's input except mine."

The immediacy and relative simplicity of "Ouch" can be very powerful as it opens the door for you to voice your perspective. It also signals that there is an issue hanging in the air that needs to be addressed. There must first be agreement and understanding between team members on the use of the "Ouch."

Could the use of "Ouch" be a possibility for you? Why or why not?

_____

_____

_____

_____

_____

Battle Plan #48 Embracing Confrontation

Confrontation can sometimes be very uncomfortable and carry real consequences, but failure to confront others is in itself a choice that comes with consequences—both real and imagined. Healthy conflict, discomfort, and confrontation are rarely easy and rarely second nature, but they are critical in initiating dialogue, sparking change, challenging the status quo, and righting wrongs.

How would you characterize your current *willingness* to confront others?

_____

_____

_____

_____

How would you characterize your current *ability* to confront others?

_____

_____

_____

_____

Describe the last time you were involved in a confrontation that you initiated?

_____

_____

_____

_____

How would you characterize your confrontation style?

_____

_____

_____

Is there anything about your confrontation style you would like to change? Why or why not?

_____

_____

_____

Who is someone (living or deceased, famous or not famous) whose confrontation style you admire?

_____

_____

_____

What specifically about the confrontation style of this person do you admire?

_____

_____

_____

_____

You can increase the likelihood of healthy confrontation that does not escalate by taking certain steps. No matter the result or outcome of the confrontation and no matter whether the person being confronted adheres to "fairness," it is important to adopt a stance that prioritizes your sense of well-being during the encounter.

- "Attack" the issue and not the person(s)

- Have a valid viewpoint

- Have confi dence and conviction in your values and beliefs

- Know what outcome you need and want

- Avoid the use of the accusatory "you"

- Assume ignorance and not malice

- Regard the person(s) as a construction site rather than a demolition site

- Allow the person(s) to maintain dignity

- Don't take a "counter-attack" personally

- Keep your voice, posture, and gestures neutral

- Be respectful but fi rm

- Clarify the distinction between intent and impact

Based on what you know about yourself, what are some other ideas?

_____

_____

_____

_____

_____

Battle Plan #49 Mentoring Your Badass Self

You can avoid lapsing into complacency, falling back into old habits and patterns, and losing your passion for the "fight" by continuing to nurture and develop your badass self. Self-mentoring is a well-known process whereby you take stock of your strengths and weaknesses as part of a plan to becoming your ideal self. The process involves a lot of "self-ing"—self-awareness, self-reflection, self-assessment, self-affirmation, self-development, self-monitoring, and so forth.

You can start by designing your own rules around self-mentoring. Using this very generic definition of mentoring as a foundation, create your own definition of self-mentoring.

Mentoring: Providing encouragement to and helping another to figure out the right life moves and/or career moves to make.

How would you define self-mentoring for *you*?

_____

_____

_____

_____

What advice would you offer yourself about entering into a mentoring relationship with you?

_____

_____

_____

_____

A badass is a confident, uncompromising-on-values person. Mentoring your badass self involves (1) being in tune with badass traits you possess and also want to nurture, (2) being in tune with badass traits you lack and also want to develop, and (3) having a plan for encouragement and development based on your definition of self-mentoring.

Review the following list of badass traits and circle the traits that you possess and also want to nurture:

- Speaks up and speaks out even when others are silent

- Doesn't care what anybody else thinks of her for speaking up and speaking out

- Takes care of and prioritizes herself

- Does the right thing even when it's unpopular or hard to do

- Challenges the status quo

- Calls out bias, inequity, injustice

- Lives by her own rules

- Doesn't give up

- Undertakes brave and courageous pursuits

- Speaks truth to power

- Takes calculated risks

- Sets and communicates boundaries

- Says "No" without fear

- Isn't swayed by detractors and haters

- Doesn't give in to peer pressure

- Speaks her mind

From among the traits that you circled, write down the ones you consider to be your strongest five and rank them starting with your strongest:

YOUR STRONGEST TRAITS

1. _____

2. _____

3. _____

4. _____

5. _____

What surprises you? Record your thoughts and insights.

_____

_____

_____

_____

_____

_____

_____

Here's the list one more time. This time, circle the traits that you lack and also want to develop:

- Speaks up and speaks out even when others are silent

- Doesn't care what anybody else thinks of her for speaking up and speaking out

- Takes care of and prioritizes herself

- Does the right thing even when it's unpopular or hard to do

- Challenges the status quo

- Calls out bias, inequity, injustice

- Lives by her own rules

- Doesn't give up

- Undertakes brave and courageous pursuits

- Speaks truth to power

- Takes calculated risks

- Sets and communicates boundaries

- Says "No" without fear

- Isn't swayed by detractors and haters

- Doesn't give in to peer pressure

- Speaks her mind

From the traits that you circled, identify five that represent the greatest opportunity for development:

YOUR GREATEST OPPORTUNITY TRAITS

1. _____

2. _____

3. _____

4. _____

5. _____

What surprises you? Record your thoughts and insights.

_____

_____

_____

_____

_____

_____

_____

Sometimes others around you can provide valuable clues about your badass self. Think about words that have been used to describe you, even the ones that offended you (for example, being called a b*tch by a man means you are assertive). The list below contains a mix of non-codified and codified descriptors and labels. Circle each that has been directed at you as a compliment or weaponized against you as a slur. Use the blank spaces to add others that aren't represented here.

brave	audacity
courageous	b*tch
grit	combative
bold	aggressive
moxie	opinionated
assertive	blunt
resilient	direct
persistent	curt
determined	unapologetic
honest	fierce
daring	controversial
strong	radical
thought-provoking	divisive
decisive	uncooperative
purposeful	non-team player
driven	brutal

What is your primary self-mentoring goal?

_____

_____

_____

_____

_____

_____

_____

How will you achieve it? Outline your plan?

_____

_____

_____

_____

_____

_____

_____

How will you hold yourself accountable?

_____

_____

_____

_____

_____

_____

What does success look like?

_____

_____

_____

_____

_____

_____

Battle Plan #50 Bettering Your "I-Sight"

Creating a signature affirmation that grounds and centers you can be one of the most powerful tools in your well-being and self-advocacy arsenal. The right affirmation will add to your sense of well-being and fuel self-advocacy.

Affirmations are especially empowering when they are easy to memorize and take to heart and when they are repeated often to yourself when you're in need of an extra dose of your inner source of power. They are called "affirmations" because they affirm you, who you are, and what you stand for. They are what you see and want to see about yourself.

Before you craft one of your own, look at these five sample affirmations.

I am worthy.
I believe in myself.
I express gratitude every day.
I am more than enough.
I will answer the question that wasn't asked.

What do you notice about the affirmations?

_____

_____

_____

_____

_____

_____

_____

Tips for designing an affirmation for yourself:

- Use your "I" voice.

- Believe it.

- Make it easy to memorize.

- Boldly declare it to yourself consistently throughout the day.

Write out your affirmation here:

_____

_____

_____

_____

_____

_____

_____

_____

Did you use your "I" voice?

Do you believe it?

Is it easy to memorize?

Can you declare it to yourself throughout the day?

Conclusion

Having better I-sight (affirmations) and having gotten your shift (purpose) together, your badass self can keep going! Why? Because you are part of the good in this world that can create more good in this world. WarriHERs aren't warriHERs because they are good at fighting; warriHERs are warriHERs because they fight for good. They fight for cause.

You are strong.
You are valuable.
You are worthy.
You are part of a mighty force of warriHERs.

Here again are ten warriHERs to encourage you and fortify you for the fight.

Because one of the lives you FIGHT for should be your own!

WarriHER Wisdom on Fighting it Forward

WarriHER Wisdom on Fighting it Forward
Baylie

In 2018, Forbes 500 companies employed 476 male CEO's, yet only 24 females. Men continuously advocate for themselves and continue to swing their d*cks in the board-room (figuratively, of course). I think women are sometimes intimidated by this and are afraid to fully vocalize how they feel in fear of the response they might get or how they will be perceived.

My biggest advice for women would be to refrain from associating self-advocacy with negative connotations like pushiness, arrogance, aggression, or greed. If you know the value of what you bring to the table and are looking for an additional 10% in compensation because of the additional responsibility you were given, say something! Do not wait for someone to acknowledge the additional work you are putting in. Make it be known.

Remember to be objective and offer solutions to any problems you are identifying. Never let yourself be complacent. If women do not speak up, they are going to continue to be overlooked. If being vocal is a challenge for you, attempt to practice with people closest to you or in the mirror so that you can get more comfortable. The more you advocate for yourself in real life, the more it will become natural for you.

WarriHER Wisdom on Fighting it Forward
Carrie

Love yourself and be honest with yourself. Don't overcomplicate this. Listen to your heart. Sometimes love and truth are tough. Expect surprises and instead of dwelling in regret, use what you find as power to overcome weakness.

Don't try to change anyone. Just focus on being YOUR best. Some people will see you come alive with vitality and joy and jump on the train with you. Others will fight it. Keep loving them without letting them influence you or an expectation of a specific outcome.

Be respected and detach yourself from your need to be liked. Truth is, some people won't like the more powerful you. Some people won't like you whether you're powerful or not. When you concern yourself with being liked you relinquish your responsibility. It's a very sneaky self-protection technique! This doesn't mean you aren't compassionate and driven by love. It means that you aren't attached to the outcome.

WarriHER Wisdom on Fighting it Forward
ChrisTiana

In my short time on this planet, I have come to a blistering understanding of the brevity of life. We often think of our time limitations in terms of years or decades, but what if we don't have that long? What would you do if you were told you only had one week left to live—or one day? How would you spend your time? I know, it's a bit morbid, but also extremely realistic. We simply don't have time to spend on anything that will not lead to liberation, joy, or a sense of accomplishment. Time is precious, and it is a privilege.

If I can impart any advice, I have learned throughout my life journey that it is finding ways to embrace the finality and absurdity of existing in time. I encourage folks to find accessible and transformative ways to lean into experimenting with failure and learning to make decisions with your time that will lead to whatever it means to you to be "well" and at peace.

WarriHER Wisdom on Fighting it Forward
Harriet

It's okay to prioritize YOU! Don't feel guilty; others prioritize themselves so why can't you prioritize YOU?! It doesn't make you selfish. I remember someone saying it was selfish when I would get regular massages when my daughter was an infant. That's just plain ignorant. Don't listen to other people. Prioritizing you makes YOU better! When you are better, you are better for others, too!!

WarriHER Wisdom on Fighting it Forward
Jemia

Love yourself first. Think about yourself first. As women, we are natural nurturers. We love to give to others regardless of what we get in return. But the biggest advice I give women, especially women who are just coming into their careers, is that you have to put yourself first. Even when you feel like you do not deserve to come first in whatever situation you are in, you do.

Nothing can be done in this world if you are not confident in what you are doing. You may get tasks or projects done, but was it done the way you know it could have been? Practice asking yourself, "How does this make me feel?" and "Will this help me get to where I am going?" before you take on more in your professional and personal life. Putting your hands in everything is not self-advocacy, and it is not self-love. You decide where you go. You decide what you can take on. There is always a choice. Make the right one. And YOU are always the right choice.

WarriHER Wisdom on Fighting it Forward
Laura

My advice is to start by being proud of yourself. Start with all you have done, not all you should do differently or wish you could change. You are here. Think of how many lives have been lived, how many odds you have beaten just to live on the earth at this exact moment. Try your best to stop comparing your life to someone else's; you are a miracle just as you are. Whether we look at our lives from a scientific, spiritual, or psychological standpoint, we are all precious and our lives valuable. You have thoughts, insights, and opinions that only you can offer the world.

I am the first in my family to finish college. Not only did I finish my bachelor's degree, but I did it with two very small children and in only one year. I then went on to earn my doctoral degree less than five years after earning my GED. I later started my own consulting firm and am currently writing two books. All the while, people told me to slow down, don't do so much, and that I wasn't smart enough/old enough/something enough to be everything I dreamed of being. I often cried, wanted to give up, or gave into believing what my antagonists were saying. It's okay to have days where you feel yourself drowning in despair. The point is not to live there. Visit and then force yourself to get up and keep moving.

Begin any endeavor by listing all you have done and all that you are good at before you ever think of what you want to do next. Wake up and go to bed every night listing what you are grateful for, even on days when that list seems terribly small. Find joy in the smallest blessings—a clean counter, running water, folded clothes, gas in your car. The more we live in a state of gratitude, personal grace, and simple joy, the greater our sense of contentment, and the better we can clarify what matters to us and who we want to be.

WarriHER Wisdom on Fighting it Forward
Mayerland

The best advice I have ever received or given has come from the one true source of wisdom, the Bible. We should all strive to be virtuous women as described in Proverbs 31:10-31.

WarriHER Wisdom on Fighting it Forward
Nani

A quote from Beyoncé that resonates with me is, "I have learned that it is no one else's job to take care of me but me."

Be kind to yourself. As women, we all tend to give so much of ourselves and then forget to refuel, replenish, and re-energize. We can be hard on ourselves if we don't achieve all we set out to do and do it perfectly. It's okay to say no sometimes. You don't have to do it all! Be intentional about doing and scheduling things that make you feel good each day. Do what you love and what brings you joy. Reflect and make mindful choices. Know what gives you energy and what drains you. You have to nurture yourself so you can continue to be your best self and be able to serve, contribute, and make a difference in the world.

Pay attention to your self-talk. Eliminate harsh, negative words to yourself. Have a go-to list of positive "I am" statements and affirmations to speak truth about yourself each day. When negative thoughts pop into your head, swap them out with your awesome "I am" statements. "Whatever is true, whatever is noble, whatever is right, whatever is pure, whatever is lovely, whatever is admirable; if anything is excellent or praiseworthy, think about such things…. [a]nd the God of peace will be with you" (Philippians 4:8-9).

Know your worth and don't accept anything less than what you deserve. If anyone (including yourself) tries to tear you down, repeat your "I am"s. Your mind and body are connected, so be mindful of your posture and your facial expression. If you think powerful thoughts, it will show outwardly.

Always be grateful. Stop to recognize the abundance of goodness in your life. Start a gratitude journal to reflect on what you are thankful for each day. Living with gratitude will change your outlook on life. "Acknowledging the good that you already have in your life is the foundation for all abundance." Eckhart Tolle.

Be your authentic self. You are all beautiful beings and you have an incredible purpose in this world. Your career, your title, or wealth doesn't define who you are. Your true identity comes from within when your character, your energy, and your beliefs are all perfectly aligned. You possess unique gifts only YOU can offer the world.

Be resilient. No matter who you are, you will have struggles and hardships in life. It's difficult to realize it at the time but in many ways, it's a gift and a blessing. If you approach it as a season of learning, growing, and thriving, you'll be ready with more resilience, endurance, perseverance, and wit to level up for the next chapter in your life. Believe that you are exactly where you are supposed to be at this moment. A life well-lived is chosen one day at a time. Keep on thriving.

WarriHER Wisdom on Fighting it Forward
Rhoda

My advice would be to take time to learn who you are, do self- discovery sessions on yourself (like the ones in this playbook!), and never allow anyone to pigeonhole you. Identity is very important; many people have an identity crisis, and the worst thing is being told who you are by someone who doesn't know who they are! When you know who you are, you recognize what you are capable of and will do great things… you will be unstoppable. Don't be afraid to go for the things you want and don't be afraid to say what you want either!

I once had the opportunity to partner with another organization. During our initial meeting with principals from the organization, it was apparent they wanted to use us, our ideas, and concepts, and not benefit who we represent! I turned down the offer to work with them because I know what my vision is and what outcome I am looking for. I know my worth and the worth of my organization. Knowing your identity gives you confidence to make decisions.

WarriHER Wisdom on Fighting it Forward
Sara

Prior to writing for this playbook, I've never really thought of myself in terms of being a woman! Like many autistic people, I don't feel like a particular gender, just Sara. I wouldn't even consider myself nonbinary although perhaps that is a generational by-product. In any event, my advice is really for anyone, and especially autistic people, who have been disassociated and dis-integrated from their true selves, regardless of the reasons.

What's worked for me is to stop and listen. Listen to the voice inside myself that is loving and kind—the voice that I would use to talk with a friend, with my son, and with my students. I would encourage everyone to take the time for themselves to be with themselves and speak kindly and "care-fully" to themselves about their own thoughts and actions.

When I'm really struggling, it's helpful to also spend time with people that are accepting and uplifting. People who will tell me the truth, and that want the best for me. These people aren't always family in the traditional sense of the word; they are people who have become family through their actions and acceptance. It's important, though, that I still filter even their words through my own beliefs and decision-making process, because I spent far too many years listening to and believing what other people thought about me and thought I should do.

In general, believe in yourself! You are wise, good, and kind beyond belief. Find the voice inside yourself that knows what's true and have a conversation.

Each of us is already equipped inside for greatness, so courageously sustain your greatness, and you'll never be the same!

Keep Going!

Appendix of WarriHER Tactics

When others talk over you...

1. Keep right on talking and don't even acknowledge the interruption.

2. Confidently say, "Bob, I'm talking." Use the offender's name and ditch words and phrases like "please," "allow me," "I'm sorry, but..." Even ditch the "excuse me."

3. Kill 'em with kindness. "Thank you, Bob, for being an enthusiastic vocal advocate of my ideas." (This is especially effective when delivered with a hint of sarcasm when your ideas have been co-opted.)

4. Create and repeat to yourself an empowerment mantra to maintain self-confidence.

5. Transform the moment through visualization and charge ahead with your voice!

6. Make a big production of packing up your things and then leave the meeting.

7. Make it hard to be talked over by speaking in a strong tone.

8. Let it roll, take a cleansing breath, and jump right back in there strong!

9. Post-meeting, approach offender(s) one-on-one to talk about it.

10. Post-meeting, approach a leader higher in status than you and the offender to talk about it.

When others try to out-talk you...

1. Suggest taking turns in order to rotate who will lead meetings.

2. Have everyone write down their input and then have each person contribute their ideas.

3. Volunteer to state your ideas in the beginning to decrease the likelihood of being missed, of time running out, or of having to interject with greater difficulty later on.

4. Suggest to the meeting leader ahead of time to create several formal intervals or checkpoints in the meeting to ensure everyone will be heard.

5. Find one male you trust, explain the situation, and turn him into your ally.

6. Tap into your inner brave badass and push yourself to talk more and talk back more.

7. Enlist the services of an external and objective group facilitator who can ensure inclusive meetings whereby each voice is heard.

8. Challenge mansplainers with, "You do realize that this is my area of expertise, right?" Also ask probing questions that challenge mansplainers and that indicate your depth of knowledge.

9. Nod. Pretend to give a damn. Repeat.

10. Dismiss or ignore the comments of overtalkers and extricate yourself with finesse and a feigned excuse.

When others overlook you...

1. Disrupt the status quo with an attention-grabbing word or phrase or novel idea.

2. Initiate a private conversation with the offender(s).

3. Enlist the advice and support of leadership.

4. Volunteer for visible assignments when it's appropriate for your circumstances to do so.

5. Seek creative ways to receive credit for your contributions.

6. Publicly and genuinely compliment your colleagues. (Giving praise when praise is due elevates your own reputation with others.)

7. Ask for feedback.

8. Evaluate your attire and make modifications, if necessary. Consider dressing as if you're the president of the company.

9. Mentor a newcomer to the team.

10. Enlist the services of a career coach.

When others judge you unfairly...

1. Turn the tables.

2. Ask clarifying questions.

3. Provide information that challenges and shatters preconceptions.

4. Invest in caring, supportive relationships and surround yourself with those who value, respect, and care about you.

5. Invest in knowing who you are.

6. Create a signature self-affirmation and repeat it often to yourself. Let it anchor you.

7. Stay positive and happy in spite of.

8. Get your inner critic in line through positive self-talk.

9. Stay focused on what and who really matters by keeping a gratitude journal.

10. Convert your known haters with kindness.

When you've been passed over...

1. P.U.S.H.: Persist Until Something Happens (and pray, if faith inclined).

2. Forge a different path to the same or better destination.

3. Report any slight to a trusted source who can do something about it.

4. Never stop advocating for yourself.

5. Leave with your skills and talent and start your own company.

6. Write down a step-by-step game plan for each goal.

7. Watch and learn the game. Then play to win.

8. Ask for feedback from a trusted advisor.

9. Seek a male sponsor with a proven track record of advocating for women.

10. Keep detailed records of your accomplishments.

When you're in overachiever mode..

1. Decide what is good enough and what needs to be more than good enough.

2. Practice delegating in small steps and progress slowly from there.

3. Institute a daily pause that gives you space to just be.

4. Woo you! Embark on a love affair with yourself.

5. Stay true to who you are with small reminders of what and who bring you joy.

6. Give yourself periodic breaks during the day to do something for just you.

7. Start using nondual thinking. You're not a success or a failure; you'll succeed in some areas and fail in others. Be okay with that.

8. Take a personal day and do no work.

9. Engage in an activity or hobby for which you have little to no skills.

10. Schedule rest on your calendar and keep the appointment.

When you're overcommitted...

1. Practice different ways to say "No" without apology.

2. Delegate.

3. Focus on only what you can control and devise strategies from there.

4. Establish clear boundaries and limits, write them down, and review them regularly!

5. When you sense you are about to overcommit, say "Stop" to yourself.

6. Schedule time with yourself and keep it!

7. Put a limit on daily commitments, track it, and hold yourself accountable.

8. Rework a commitment you don't want with one you do.

9. Team up with a support and accountability buddy with similar challenges.

10. Play hooky from work for a day and do anything you want.

When you're too accommodating...

1. Stop apologizing so much.

2. Get very real about the distinction between compromise and surrender.

3. Is there a positive WIIFM (What's in it for me?) element? If not, rework or abandon?

4. Treat you like you treat your best client/customer.

5. Confidently express your needs.

6. Choose more discriminately between minimums and maximums.

7. Implement a balanced give-and-take philosophy.

8. Start journaling your needs and wants.

9. Set priorities and limits.

10. Create an affirmation that you say to yourself when you feel susceptible.

When you're isolating yourself and going at it alone...

1. Forge friendships with women in similar positions.

2. Join a social group or online chat group.

3. Ask for and accept help from family and friends.

4. Plan a girls' night out or a girls' vacation.

5. Put the same energy into building your personal network of support as you do your professional network.

6. Be with the people you're with.

7. Practice HALT: don't get too hungry, angry, lonely, tired.

8. Set a personal goal impossible to achieve alone.

9. Volunteer at a homeless shelter.

10. Perform a random act of kindness for a neighbor at work or at home.

When you want to support women...

1. Speak up and speak out in meetings where you see gender bias happening.

2. Publicly commend the ideas and achievements of women to others.

3. Cross-mentor women in an earlier stage of their career.

4. Sponsor another woman.

5. Create a scholarship fund or sponsor an internship for women.

6. Groom a woman to take on your position when you leave or are promoted.

7. Foster friendships, not just working relationships, with other women.

8. Endorse a woman for an open position you know about.

9. Create a women's network or join an existing one.

10. Affirm women on their inner self and not their appearance.

When you want to enlist men...

1. Invite a male friend or colleague to an event that promotes women's interests.

2. Publicly commend the ideas and achievements of women to others.

3. Seek to be mentored and be a mentor to men.

4. Host a lunch-and-learn and invite women and men.

5. Enlist male colleagues to create safe spaces for women to be heard.

6. Challenge men in the workplace to take the Male Advocacy Profile quiz at http://ywomen.biz/male-advocacy-profile/#survey .

7. Lobby to get Gender Conversation Quickstarter on the meeting agenda.

8. Share with a male colleague a story that personalizes gender disparity.

9. Ask a male colleague to write a commendation letter for your files.

10. Ask men to join a workplace task force to create women-friendly policies.

About Theresa M. Robinson

With over 700 speaking engagements since 2005, Theresa is an ATD certified Master Trainer and professional speaker with international experience on six of seven continents. She is sought out by organizations seeking to unlock 100% of available talent using 3D Transformation™.

Her 3D method puts the individual first:

- Discover your purpose

- Design your own rules

- Dedicate yourself to a plan

Theresa challenges, encourages, motivates and activates others at their primal core, ignites their purpose so they can truly thrive at work and at home. Indeed, there's nothing more powerful than fully harnessing individual energy and talents to actually make a difference. In teaching smart strategies to "own your life," she helps organizations to create a permanent can-do culture of well-being and belonging on an individual, team and global level, for the long term. Everyone experiences a win-win.

In addition to well-being, DEI, physical wellness, work-life fit, gender equity, DiSC, performance coaching, keynote speaking and presenting, Theresa is adept at guiding others to embrace the "un" in uncomfortable.

She's also been known to help adults rediscover the unbridled childhood joys of jump roping, cartwheeling, and hula-hooping – and to laugh her ass off!

Debuting in 2020, is her "Well Being for Life™" course which builds on her 3D Transformation™ process.

Contact her at tmr@mastertrainertmr.com.

For more information and to schedule a workshop, contact general manager Mark Robinson at info@mastertrainertmr.com.

WarriHER & CollabHERator Invitation

WarriHER
Co-Authors

Baylie Robinson

Carrie Sechel

ChrisTiana ObeySumner

Harriet K. Harty

Jemia Young

WELL-BEING & INCLUSION CATALYST
FACILITATOR / SPEAKER / COACH / AUTHOR
Theresa M. Robinson

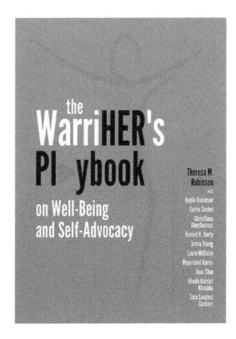

WarriHER
Co-Authors

Laura McGuire

Mayerland Harris

Nani Shin

Rhoda Harriet Khataba

Sara Sanders Gardner

If you found value in the WarriHER's Playbook on Well-Being and Self Advocacy, please consider these ideas for passing it on and continuing the momentum needed for real change:

- Join our LinkedIn women's group, WarriHERs & CollabHERators to share, reflect, support, collaborate and armor up for LIFE.

- Create your own small support group of warriHERs and collabHERators.

- Recommend and/or gift this book to other warriHERs.

- Post a review and comment on social media and Amazon.

We look forward to you joining us in the fight for your life.

Always put
your happiness FIRST!
- BR

You are the
one you have been
waiting for. You are your
ancestor's dreams made flesh
~ Dr. Laura McGuire

Be more concerned if
you can live with your
decisions, than if
everybody else can.
Carrie Seckel

Courageously
follow your heart.
It knows the way.
TMR

Be an inspiring,
striving force - Unstoppable!
Never deny yourself the
beauty of being YOU!
Harriet

Your Real self is found bey.
Your insecurities, doubts and
fears.
Rt

Be kind to yourself
your inner beauty
is a gift to the world!
D. Nani Shin

Every positive thought
is a silent prayer which will
Change your life!
Mayerland

Remember only you
own control how
bright your light
can shine

Made in the USA
Coppell, TX
13 February 2020

15744904R00142